HOMEMA
HEALTHY DOG FOOD

GUIDE + COOKBOOK with 150 Delicious Meals and Treats for Your Dog Health and Happiness. Easy, Balanced, and Picky-Eater-Proof Recipes with Raw Options Included

TIMI FOSTER

Copyright © 2023 Timi Foster. All rights reserved.

It is not legal in any way to reproduce, duplicate, or transmit any part of this document in either electronic means or printed format. Recording or copying of this publication is strictly prohibited and any storage of this document is not allowed unless with written permission from the publisher.

Limit of Liability/Disclaimer of Warranty: The Publisher and the author make no warranties with respect to the completeness and accuracy of the contents of this work. The Publisher and the author disclaim any responsibility to any person or entity for any liability, damage or loss caused directly or indirectly as a result of the use, application, or interpretation of the information presented in this work. All the nutritional information contained in this book is provided for informational purposes only. The nutritional information is based on the specific brands, measurements, and ingredients used in the recipe. Therefore, the nutritional information in this work in no way is intended to be a guarantee of the actual nutritional value of the recipe made by the reader. The publisher and the author will not be responsible for any damages resulting from the reader's reliance on nutritional information.

BONUS

7 NATURAL WAYS TO PAMPER YOUR FURRY FRIEND
The Natural Approach: a Guide to Nurturing Your Dog

DOWNLOAD YOUR GIFT NOW

Navigate to the final page of the book and **SCAN** the **QR CODE** to download the **FREE BONUS**

TABLE OF CONTENTS

INTRODUCTION ... 7
- The History of Processed Dog Food ... 8
- Benefits of Homemade Food ... 9

MAKING THE SWITCH TO HOMEMADE DOG FOOD ... 10
- BARF Diet ... 10
- PMR Diet ... 10
- Homemade Cooked ... 11
- What Vets and Nutritionists Say ... 12
- The Importance of a Gradual Transition ... 12

THE ART OF BALANCE ... 13
- **How To Create a Well-Rounded Diet** ... 13
  - *Essential Nutrients* ... 13
  - *Veggies* ... 13
  - *Fruits* ... 13
  - *Offal/Organs* ... 13
  - *Supplements and Superfoods* ... 14
  - *Crushed eggshells* ... 14
  - *Green tripe* ... 15
  - *Feeding Bones* ... 15
  - *Treats and Training Snacks* ... 15
- **What to Eat and What to Avoid** ... 16
  - *Top 10 Toxic Ingredients to Avoid* ... 16
- **Feeding Guidelines & Calorie Calculation** ... 17
- **Homemade Food Portion Guide** ... 19

FREQUENTLY ASKED QUESTIONS ... 20
- Cooking for your dog: Is it cost-effective? ... 20
- Does cooking for your dog take a lot of time? ... 20
- Storing Dog Food: Tips and Common Mistakes ... 20

COOKBOOK ... 21
SOUP RECIPES ... 21
- Beef & Beet Soup ... 22
- Lamb & Carrot Soup ... 22
- Chicken & Veggie Soup ... 23
- Chicken & Parsnip Soup ... 23
- Veggie Mix Soup ... 24

LOW-FAT PUPLOAF RECIPES ... 25
- Chicken & Carrot ... 26
- Chicken & Sweet Potato ... 26
- Chicken & Pumpkin ... 27
- Chicken & Beetroot ... 27
- Chicken & Veggie Mix 1 ... 28
- Chicken & Veggie Mix 2 ... 28
- Chicken & Veggie Mix 3 ... 29
- Chicken & Veggie Mix 4 ... 29
- Chicken & Blueberry ... 30
- Super Lean Chicken & Carrot ... 30
- Duck & Carrot ... 31
- Duck & Chicken ... 31
- Duck & Veggie Mix ... 32
- Beef, Tripe & Carrot ... 32
- Beef, Tripe & Sweet Potato ... 33
- Beef, Tripe & Pumpkin ... 33
- Beef, Tripe & Beetroot ... 34
- Beef, Tripe & Veggie Mix 1 ... 34
- Beef, Tripe & Veggie Mix 2 ... 35
- Beef & Carrot ... 35
- Beef & Sweet Potato ... 36
- Lamb & Carrot ... 36
- Lamb & Sweet Potato ... 37
- Chicken & Beef ... 37
- Chicken, Lamb & Beef ... 38
- Chicken & Kangaroo ... 38
- Beef & Kangaroo ... 39
- Super Lean Kangaroo & Carrot ... 39
- Super Lean Kangaroo & Sweet Potato ... 40
- Turkey & Apple ... 40
- Rabbit & Carrot ... 41
- Rabbit & Pumpkin ... 41
- Rabbit & Chicken ... 42
- Rabbit & Apple ... 42
- Pork, Chicken & Pumpkin ... 43

PUPLOAF RECIPES ... 44
- Chicken, Carrot & Rice ... 45
- Chicken, Sweet Potato & Millet ... 45
- Chicken, Pumpkin & Buckwheat ... 46
- Chicken, Beetroot & Brown Rice ... 46
- Chicken, Veggie & Rice ... 47
- Chicken, Veggie & Buckwheat ... 47
- Chicken, Veggie & Brown Rice ... 48
- Chicken, Root Veggies & Rice ... 48
- Chicken, Berry & Millet ... 49
- Lean Chicken & Rice ... 49
- Duck, Carrot & Buckwheat ... 50
- Poultry & Rice ... 50
- Duck, Pumpkin, Sweet Potato & Rice ... 51
- Beef, Carrot & Brown Rice ... 51
- Beef, Sweet Potato & Rice ... 52
- Beef, Pumpkin & Rice ... 52
- Beef, Beetroot & Buckwheat ... 53
- Beef, Veggies & Rice ... 53
- Beef, Beetroot, Sweet Potato & Rice ... 54
- Lean Beef, Carrot & Rice ... 54
- Lean Beef, Sweet Potato & Millet ... 55
- Rabbit, Carrot & Brown Rice ... 55
- Rabbit, Pumpkin & Buckwheat ... 56

Rabbit, Chicken & Millet	56
Rabbit, Apple & Brown Rice	57
Lamb & Grains	57
Lean Lamb, Carrot & Rice	58
Lean Lamb, Sweet Potato & Rice	58
Lamb, Salmon & Rice	59
Lamb, Salmon & Brown Rice	59
Lamb, Salmon & Millet	60
Lamb, Salmon & Buckwheat	60
Goat, Venison & White Rice	61
LAMB, Venison & Quinoa	61
Duck, Salmon & Millet	62
Chicken & Grains	62
Venison & Grains	63
Chicken, Beef & Buckwheat	63
Meat Mix & White Rice	64
Turkey, Apple & White Rice	64
Salmon, Carrot & Brown Rice	65
Pork, Chicken & Buckwheat	65
Chicken, Kangaroo & White Rice	66
Bison, Beetroot & Brown Rice	66
Bison, Carrot & White Rice	67
Beef, Bison, Egg & Barley	67
Beef, Bison & Barley	68
Beef, Kangaroo & Barley	68
Beef, Kangaroo & White Rice	69
Goat, Chicken & White Rice	69
Chicken, Sardine & Brown Rice	70
Turkey, Chicken & Millet	70
Turkey, Beef & Barley	71
Duck, Beef & Millet	71
Pork, Sardine & Brown Rice	72
Pork & Grains	72
Pork, Salmon & Rice	73
Chicken, Kangaroo & Brown Rice	73
Ostrich, Beetroot & Brown Rice	74
Ostrich, Chicken & Millet	74
Ostrich, Salmon & Brown Rice	75
Ostrich, Beef & Brown Rice	75
Ostrich, Lamb & Brown Rice	76
Chicken, Venison & White Rice	76
Beef, Venison & White Rice	77
Duck, Venison & Millet	77
Chicken, Apple & White Rice	78
Beef, Apple & Brown Rice	78
Lamb, Apple & White Rice	79
Bison, Apple & White Rice	79
Goat, Beef & Brown Rice	80
Goat, Lamb & Brown Rice	80
Goat, Salmon & Buckwheat	81
Goat, Rabbit & White Rice	81
Lean Kangaroo, Carrot & White Rice	82

KIBBLE RECIPES	**83**
Veggie Lover Kibble	84
Beef & Blueberry Kibble	84
Pumpkin Kibble	85
Carrot & Sweet Potato Kibble	85
Chicken & Apple Kibble	86
TREATS RECIPES	**87**
Banana & Peanut Butter Treat	88
Pumpkin & Oats Treat	88
Simple Peanut Butter Treat	89
Beef Dog Treat	89
Lamb Dog Treat	90
Salmon Dog Treat	90
Peanut Butter & Broth Dog Biscuit	91
Sweet & "Spicy" Chips	91
Oat & Apple Treat	92
Pumpin & Oats Treat	92
Overnight Oats for Dogs	93
Sweet Potato & Carrot Treat	93
Meat Lover Treat	94
Salmon & Pumpkin Dog Treat	94
Salmon & Carrot Dog Treat	95
Lamb & Carrot Treat	95
Chicken & Sweet Potato Treat	96
Fruit Mix Puree	96
Blueberry Cookies	97
Yogurt & Bacon Dog Biscuit	97
FROZEN TREATS RECIPES	**98**
Frozen Banana	99
Peanut butter & Banana	99
Pumpkin & Banana	100
Frozen Hen Soup	100
Frozen Spirulina Cube	101
DESSERT RECIPES	**102**
Beetroot Pancake	103
Ham & Egg Pudding	103
Bacon & Pear	104
Berry Ice Cream	104
Dog Friendly Protein Jelly	105
CONCLUSION	**106**
METRIC CONVERSION CHART	**107**
BONUS	**108**

Dear reader, first of all, thank you very much for your interest in this book, and congratulations for taking the first step towards making your dog(s) diet more natural, balanced, and healthier with fresh food. There are many misleading pieces of information about dog nutrition online, and the creation of this book was driven by the urge to provide reliable, valuable, and practical information that puts nothing else but the dogs' needs into focus.

In the following pages, you will find an overview of canine nutrition, including the history of processed dog food, the different diet types, the steps of transition from processed food to fresh food, the essential nutrients and supplements, and other interesting facts about why and how fresh dog food can benefit your furry friend. Moreover, you will learn about what to feed and what to avoid when it comes to ingredients, how to calculate your dog's daily calorie needs, and much more.

No more confusion in pet food stores. After reading this book, you will be more confident in determining what your dog should or shouldn't eat, you will find it much easier to search for ingredients and supplements, and most importantly, you will be able to produce balanced and nutrient-rich homemade dog food. It's easier and less time-consuming than you think.

If you are a pet parent and your dog suffers from allergies, intolerances, or any other nutrition-related condition, or gets bored of processed food easily, or if you just simply want to improve the diet of your canine companion, this book is for you.

DISCLAIMER

Please be aware that this book provides general information about pet health and well-being, but it is not meant to be a substitute for veterinary care. It is important to consult your veterinarian before making any changes to your dog's diet, especially if your pet has health issues.

If your dog has medical conditions, you may need to adjust specific diets recommended by veterinarians. Ask your vet about your dog's unique nutritional requirements and consider seeking advice from a certified veterinary nutritionist. The author and contributors of this book cannot be held responsible for any issues or consequences arising from the improper implementation of the information and/or recipes provided herein.

INTRODUCTION

The digestive system of dogs has undergone significant changes since domestication. As a result, the dietary needs of modern-day dogs may differ from those of their ancestors. Some behaviors of your four-legged friend that may seem peculiar are actually rooted in centuries of evolution and perfectly natural.

You may have wondered at some point why dogs eat so fast and seem incredibly voracious sometimes… It's because they **cannot move their jaws sideways** like herbivores, consequently they cannot chew food thoroughly. But don't worry, that's absolutely normal. Dogs' teeth are designed to catch the prey, tear it to pieces, and pass those towards the esophagus. This is exactly what they do with the food they find in their bowl. Their **stomach is extremely acidic** (pH is around 1-2) and it helps to break down meat and bones, and to kill any unwanted bacteria.

A curious question: have you ever seen your dog grab a piece of dried chew from under the ground that was hidden there for weeks or even months? Don't worry, it's normal, and yes, dogs can digest seemingly rotten food, but that doesn't mean they can be fed rotten food. For instance, **moldy food is dangerous and highly toxic for dogs**, so it's important to pay attention to these details when feeding your furry friend.

Back to dogs' digestive system: dogs gain energy mainly from **protein, fat, and carbohydrates**. Yes, carbs. During the past few centuries, the majority of dogs got leftovers as their main food source, and leftovers included carbs. That is why dogs' digestive system slowly but surely adapted to the new conditions, and their small intestine began to produce an enzyme called amylase. This enzyme is responsible for the digestion of carbohydrates, and this means dogs – in small amounts – can digest carbs. Some say it's not recommended to add carbohydrates – even minimally – to dogs' diets, but we should take into account the evolution of the canine digestive system, and the long history dogs have lived alongside us. However, the two most important macronutrients our canine friends require on a daily basis are protein and fat.

Having a good understanding of these aspects is crucial. It helps us better comprehend certain behaviors of our furry friends, alleviates concerns about their seemingly peculiar habits, and empowers us to confidently decide to switch to homemade dog food with custom-tailored recipes. This decision is not only motivated by the importance of feeding them a diet free from preservatives and fillers, but also by our knowledge of their specific needs and a deeper understanding of how our best friend has evolved in virtue of the history we have shared in past centuries.

THE HISTORY AND EVOLUTION OF PROCESSED DOG FOOD

One of the first questions that pops into pet parents' minds when a dog arrives to the family is "What type of kibble and canned food should I buy?". And this is not a coincidence. Over the past half century, processed dog food production has become one of the largest industries in the world. But what exactly is processed dog food? It may sound surprising but **kibbles were born out of necessity** after the world wars. Due to famine and shortage of meat there was a need for an easily-accessible, yet cheap dog food, so dogs were fed with biscuit-like food – let's say the "ancestor" of dry dog food we know today – that was high in cereals. Besides the low price, one of the main advantages of this food type was **convenience,** therefore it became increasingly popular among dog owners, and its popularity still prevails. Thanks to this, along with effective marketing strategies, nowadays we don't even think about any other food types: dogs eat kibble and canned dog food, period.

While we are trying to find healthy, organic, and fresh ingredients for ourselves, our dogs live on highly processed, extruded kibbles. It's quite contradictory, isn't it?

Wait a second, what does "extruded" mean? The cheapest and easiest method to produce dry dog food is through a process called extrusion. **During this process, the food mixture goes through a die that gives its shape, and the mixture is heated to extremely high temperatures – around 200 °C – several times.** It's obvious that no beneficial macro-, and micronutrients can survive in such a hostile environment. To regain the lost elements, **artificial macronutrients and vitamins are added** to the food. When the food is ready, there comes another step: preservation. In order to prevent the decay of kibble and make it last for months, huge amounts of **preservatives** are needed. The two synthetic preservatives that are often used in processed dog food are **BHT (Butylated Hydroxytoluene) and BHA (Butylated Hydroxyanisole).** Their waxy texture makes them suitable for preventing kibbles from falling apart, and for making them last longer.

Interestingly, **canned dog food** has a bit longer history than kibble, as they have been available for nearly a hundred years. The main reason for their popularity is the same as of kibble: convenience. It's so easy to pop open a can and fill the dog bowl, isn't it? On the label of canned dog food, you often see expressions like "meat and meat byproducts," "meat and animal derivatives," which can be quite confusing if you are looking for food for a dog with allergies or intolerances, for example. Why? Because in most cases the exact **ingredients are not identifiable.** Another important aspect of canned dog food is the can itself, more precisely the material used during production. Most cans are lined with plastic that often contains a chemical called **BPA (bisphenol A),** which – according to the FDA – can leak into the food stored in the can, and BPA is really the last of the ingredients you would want to add to your beloved four-legged friend's meal.

One might ask what's the difference between dry and wet dog food in terms of ingredients, additives and production methods.

Well, generally speaking – compared to kibble – canned food is considered less processed, may be less in calories and carbs, does not dehydrate dogs, and is more digestible. Each dog is different and it's always the pet parents' decision what they buy for their furry friends, but one thing is for sure: dogs do much better on food made of natural ingredients, and you will see why.

BENEFITS OF HOMEMADE FOOD

Improved digestion, more energy, shiny coat, healthy weight? It's all possible with natural, fresh homemade dog food.

Unlike processed food, homemade dog food is completely transparent. What does this mean? It means that **you know exactly what goes into your dog's bowl**, and you have total **control over the ingredients** you use. Consequently, you can make your dog's diet more **varied, balanced** and full of yummy natural ingredients. Another big advantage of homemade dog food is that you don't need artificial additives, preservatives, coloring, and flavor enhancers. Why? Because dogs love the smell of freshly-made, natural dog food.

Moreover, feeding your pet with natural ingredients **can be less expensive**, and most importantly, you can **say goodbye to nutrition-related allergies and intolerances** with the help of homemade food and elimination diets. Don't worry, we will talk about this later in more detail. Just like in the case of humans, **each dog is different** and each dog has specific needs. The good news is that after learning a few basic techniques, with the help of this book, you will be able to provide food for your canine companions that is tailored to their needs.

CHAPTER 1
MAKING THE SWITCH TO HOMEMADE DOG FOOD

Finding the best diet for your furbaby is a demanding task, and there are so many products and pieces of information online that can create confusion in pet parents. After reading this chapter, you will have a better understanding of the different dog diet types, and you will be more confident when it comes to ingredient selection. In this section you will find more details about BARF, PMR, and HOMEMADE diets, which can be perfect alternatives to canned or dry dog food – if given with care. Let's start getting familiar with the most well-known diets to learn more and make an informed choice. For example, you could decide to adopt them for short periods based on your dog's different needs, taking the best from each of them.

BARF DIET

You've probably heard of the BARF (**Biologically Appropriate Raw Food**) diet. As its name suggests, this diet is focusing on species-appropriate nutrition. BARF is becoming very popular nowadays, but it is important to emphasize that it does NOT mean feeding your dog raw meat and nothing else! Providing an unbalanced diet for your furry friend can lead to serious nutrient deficiencies and health issues. The BARF diet consists of fresh, uncooked ingredients like muscle meat, fat, edible bones, organs, vegetables, natural supplements, and seeds and fruit occasionally. The standard ratio for BARF feeding is the following: **70% muscle meat, 10% raw edible bone, 5% liver, 5% other secreting organs** (for example kidney and spleen), **7% vegetables, 2% seeds or nuts, and 1% fruit.** Remember that even though the heart and lungs are organs, they should be considered as meat in the BARF diet.

In this book, you will find a good number of balanced recipes in the cookbook section where the raw option is included and indicated if you wish to try feeding your dog in this way.

PMR DIET

PMR stands for Prey Model Raw feeding. Similarly to BARF, this diet focuses on the natural food that dogs consume in the wilderness. In other words, it mimics the diet of your canine companion's ancestors. The main difference between BARF and PMR is that the Prey Model Raw diet consists of whole prey feeding without any plant or herbal ingredients. Some of the most popular whole prey are fish (for instance Mackerel and sardine), pheasant and rabbit.

You might have heard about the **80/10/10 feeding ratio:** 80% meat, 10% organs (preferably secreting organs) and 10% raw bones. That is exactly the main structure of PMR. However, it's important to emphasize that PMR is not suitable for every dog, and it **is not considered a complete diet** due to the lack of vegetables and other essential supplements. If given alone, it may lead to nutritional deficiencies in the long term; however, when supplemented with vegetables and necessary vitamins and minerals, the PMR diet can improve oral health, skin and coat health, and provide more energy. The PMR diet is often suggested by veterinarians as an elimination diet to be strictly followed for 8-10 weeks in case dogs exhibit intolerances or allergies. In practice, for a limited period, the dog receives only one source of protein - usually a protein source that the dog has never eaten before - in this way, gradually reintroducing other ingredients makes it easier to identify and eliminate the element that is causing the unwanted reaction of the body.

Attention:
Naturally, when opting for raw ingredients, it is important to purchase meat from a reliable source and handle it with care. Proper handling of raw ingredients helps prevent potential bacterial infections and cross-contamination. For example, it is recommended to use different cutting boards, one for meat and one for vegetables, to thoroughly clean kitchen surfaces, and to take normal precautions that we use when cooking for ourselves.

Pro tip: it's possible to combine BARF and PMR. You can give your dog bigger pieces of meat or whole prey but it should always be done under supervision to avoid choking hazard.

HOMEMADE COOKED

There are many misunderstandings about feeding our dogs raw meat, mostly stemming from a misconception of the diet. Feeding a raw meat diet does not mean providing our dogs with 100% protein, but rather ensuring a well-balanced mix of nutrients. It's important to keep in mind that regularly feeding large amounts of meat can lead to issues, particularly in medium and large breeds. Additionally, reducing the amount of meat is recommended for dogs with allergies or intolerances. And this is when **homemade cooked dog food** comes into the picture as a great, natural alternative to raw diet types. Believe it or not, some dogs do not like raw ingredients or cannot digest them properly for various reasons. Furthermore, some pet parents prefer to stay on the "safe" side in terms of unwanted bacteria associated with the **improper preparation and handling** of raw ingredients.

One of the main advantages of homemade cooked food is that you can **customize it according to your dog's individual needs,** and, most importantly, **you know exactly what goes into the dog's bowl.** It is as simple as that! With the combination of meat, veggies, high-quality grains like brown rice, buckwheat and quinoa–you can choose to go grain-free as well–, and superfoods, you can say goodbye to additives and preservatives forever. The fear of bacteria is over and you will be amazed by the results. Moreover, your furry friend will never get bored of the food.

WHAT VETS AND NUTRITIONISTS SAY ABOUT HOMEMADE DOG FOOD

You may wonder why many vets and nutritionists advise against homemade dog food. The **problem is not the homemade food itself, but the ingredients and the way the food is given to the dog.** Inappropriate feeding and potentially harmful ingredients can lead to nutrient deficiencies, and can cause life-threatening situations. So, before making any changes on the dog's diet, pet parents should educate themselves and **ask their vets and nutritionists** about the needs of dog's digestive system.

Vets and nutrition specialists all agree that **homemade food**–if it is complete, balanced, and given with care–**can do wonders with dogs**, especially with pups who suffer from processed food-related allergies and intolerances.

As you can see, feeding your dog is not "black or white," there are no "good" or "bad" diets. **Finding the balance and taking your dog's individual needs into account** is the key to a happy and healthy pup tummy.

MAKE IT SAFE: THE IMPORTANCE OF A GRADUAL TRANSITION

Different types of diets require **different digestive environments.** Among all the food, processed food–especially kibbles–puts the most stress on the digestive system. This is why it is not recommended to feed dry dog food with raw or cooked food at the same time for an extended period of time, in order to avoid overloading your dog's stomach. If you decide to switch from processed food to homemade, do it gradually within a short timeframe to avoid putting excessive strain on your pet's digestive system. Try to increase the ratio of "new food" by 20-25% every day, while reducing the amount of "old food" accordingly. The ideal transition period is one week, and it should not exceed two weeks. Remember, the primary objective of a gradual transition is to minimize stress on your dog's digestive system.

During the transition phase–and whenever you want to help dogs' digestive system–it's recommended to add **pre-, and probiotics, or natural probiotics, for example fermented herbs** to your dog's diet. They come in capsule, powder, or liquid form so you can easily hide it in your pup's meal.

Although this rarely happens, it's possible that some dogs, especially picky eaters, will not touch the "new food." Don't worry; it's totally normal. A dog who has always been fed kibble will not recognize homemade food as food at the beginning. In most cases, it is enough to be patient and persistent, but the good news is you can help, too. For example, hand feeding is a great way to overcome the introductory period, and it builds trust. You can use a yummy treat as a reward when the dog starts to eat the homemade food. Positive reinforcement helps them understand that this type of food is good.

CHAPTER 2
THE ART OF BALANCE

HOW TO CREATE A WELL-ROUNDED DIET

The most important thing is that we should provide appropriate food for dogs' needs, and find the correct balance. In this section you will find plenty of useful pieces of information about **what dogs can eat, why they should eat specific food items, and what they should avoid.** By the end of this chapter, you will understand the importance of each ingredient, and you will be ready to create your pup's first homemade meal. Satisfaction guaranteed!

ESSENTIAL NUTRIENTS
Similarly to humans, the six most important nutrients for dogs are **water, protein, carbohydrates, fat, vitamins, and minerals.** The most important vitamins are Vitamin A, Vitamin E, Vitamin D, Vitamin K, B-complex, Phosphorus, and Calcium. You may wonder why Vitamin C is not on the list. The good news is healthy dogs do not need **vitamin C** supplements because **they can synthesize it** in the liver. If a dog's meal includes all the above-mentioned nutrients in adequate amounts, the diet is complete and balanced.

VEGGIES
Dogs are **not obligate carnivores** like cats, and if we want to follow the "what dogs find in the wild" concept, it is important for them to **add veggies** to their diet. Dogs often ate **roots and herbs** in the wild–not to mention the herbs in their prey's stomach–, and recent research says dogs are more like **scavengers.** Of course, veggies shouldn't be given in huge amounts, BUT fiber intake helps them a lot as it can help the digestive system.

FRUITS
Feeding fruit in large amounts and/or on a regular basis is not recommended due to their **sugar content.** Occasionally some **apples, blueberries, and bananas** are fine, but it's important to keep the amount of fruit low.

OFFAL/ORGANS
Offal and organs in general are **great sources of vitamins,** but **should be given in moderation** because they (especially secreting organs like the liver) contain huge amounts of vitamin A and D and it's **easy to overdose** them, if given in large amounts.

SUPPLEMENTS AND SUPERFOODS

Supplements are necessary for dogs on raw or cooked homemade diets. They make the meal balanced and they are **packed with beneficial nutrients.** It's important to use **100% natural** supplements because they tend to be easier to absorb.

The most important supplements are **dried rosehip powder, salmon oil, linseed oil, spirulina, brown seaweed, green-lipped mussel powder, collagen, powdered bone, powdered eggshell, and Brewer's yeast.** Rosehip powder is full of powerful antioxidants that can support the immune system, and it also facilitates the absorption of joint supplements, like collagen and MSMS if given at the same time. Salmon oil should be given for 2 months max. That is followed by a 2-month pause, because if given long-term, salmon oil can block Vitamin E absorption. The same applies to rosehip powder. Similarly to salmon oil, Brewer's yeast and linseed oil can **support skin and coat health,** and are great alternatives for salmon oil-pause periods. Green-lipped mussel powder, collagen, powdered bone, and powdered eggshell are **natural joint supplements** and they can support the proper development and functioning of joints and hips, especially for large and giant breeds. Powdered bone and powdered eggshell are great alternatives if you do not feed bones. They are natural **calcium** sources. Spirulina is an excellent supplement in case of allergies and/or digestive issues. And when you use it, don't worry about the color of the food, even a small amount can turn a whole meal green. **Brown seaweed** can also support skin and coat health, but it contains huge amounts of **iodine** and is not recommended for dogs who have or are prone to thyroid issues.

Did you know there are superfoods for dogs too? Actually, **there are many dog-friendly superfoods.** Here are some of the most nutritionally-dense ones: **salmon, broccoli, beetroot, sweet potato, pumpkin, blueberry, coconut oil, fermented veggies, and kefir/yogurt.** All of them contain essential nutrients and are full of **antioxidants.** Salmon, sweet potato, and pumpkin can contribute to **healthy skin and coat,** broccoli, beetroot, and blueberry have detoxifying and anti-inflammatory properties, **coconut oil can provide relief for itchy skin** on the outside, and fermented veggies, kefir, and yogurt can support the proper functioning of the digestive system.

CRUSHED EGGSHELLS

Crushed eggshells can be a simple and common way to provide calcium to dogs. In fact, the shell of a medium-sized egg contains approximately 750-800 mg of calcium. It is important to **consult with your veterinarian to determine your dog's daily calcium requirement,** as this can vary based on factors such as the amount of meat in their diet, their size, and their age. For instance, puppies generally require higher amounts of calcium. **Preparing this natural and homemade supplement is quite simple.** The only precaution you need to take is to sterilize the shells to eliminate any bacteria before grinding them. To do this, simply place the shells in an oven at a temperature of 140°/150° for about 10 minutes. Once cooled, you can finely grind them using a blender or coffee grinder. Alternatively, you can also use the shells of boiled eggs, ensuring they are well-dried before pulverizing them.
The resulting eggshell powder can be stored in a glass jar and kept in the refrigerator for approximately 15 days. To collect enough eggshells, you can freeze them in a bag each time you use eggs in the kitchen, after washing and drying them.

GREEN TRIPE

All the supplements and superfoods mentioned above can be beneficial for your pup, but this special food item deserves a paragraph of its own. The name may sound strange but green tripe is a wonderful ingredient. It's called green because it is **unbleached and contains half-digested grass.** This organ is **full of beneficial digestive enzymes** which can support dogs' digestive system. Basically it's full of **natural probiotics** and is highly recommended for dogs on a homemade diet.

FEEDING BONES

Bone contains **essential calcium** your furry friend's body needs. Maintaining a correct **calcium to phosphorus ratio** is extremely important to proper development. For a healthy adult dog, the calcium-phosphorus **ratio is 1:1.** Excess calcium and phosphorus is excreted by the kidneys and eliminated from the dog's body. Neither of these puts unwanted stress on the kidneys of healthy dogs, but if the dog has kidney problems, phosphorus intake should be checked regularly.

As you can see, feeding bones to dogs is necessary and possible, of course, but **it should be done with care.** First of all, you should never give cooked/baked bones to your pup, because they can break easily. **Sharp bone fragments** can damage the throat or pierce the esophagus, and they can cause injuries on the lining of the stomach and intestines as well. If you do not grind bones together with raw meat, it's essential to **provide bones separately from the rest of the food** to avoid any issues, and **always under supervision.** If you provide bones separately, try to give **bones that have meat chunks** on. Why? Because meat chunks on bones help to protect intestines during the digestion process. Feeding **excessive amounts** of bones can lead to **intestinal blockage** and cause life-threatening situations which require surgical intervention. The feeding of large, weight-bearing bones–even when raw–is strictly prohibited. According to the general guideline, one or two raw bones per week is a good starting point, while paying attention to the dog's feces. Chicken bones and rib bones are usually not recommended, but every dog is different. When it comes to feeding bones, **size matters the most.** The bone should be bigger than what your dog could easily swallow, so it should be longer than their head. In most cases, beef marrow bones, lamb shanks, and brisket bones are fine. Among these three bone types, marrow bones are the easiest to produce splinters, due to their structure, but the general rule applies for all kinds of bones: they **should always be fed under supervision.**

TREATS AND TRAINING SNACKS

Training snacks and treats should all be **organic and 100% natural.** For example, dogs love **dried rabbit ears,** horse skin, or cow ears with or without fur. Did you know? Furry treats can act like a "broom" and clean the walls of the intestines. The natural treat list is endless, but it is important to take your furry friend's health issues and intolerances (if any) into account when choosing these. When it comes to natural treats and chews, **size also matters!** Large dogs need bigger chews, small breeds need smaller chews to avoid choking hazard. One of the best natural chews is **coffee wood:** it's hard and dense, but only tiny, soft pieces are produced when chewed, and it does not damage the enamel. Don't worry, it does not contain caffeine.

WHAT TO EAT AND WHAT TO AVOID

There are many ingredients that are safe for your four-legged friend. Some of the most popular dog-friendly food items are **carrot, white rice, brown rice, buckwheat, quinoa, plain, unsweetened yogurt, salmon, fish, all kinds of meat (yes, your pup can eat kangaroo meat, too!), blueberries, banana, cucumber, apple (without the core), watermelon (without seeds), beetroot, pumpkin, and broccoli.** You might have heard about **chocolate** as one of the most toxic ingredients for dogs. In most cases, the severity of symptoms depends on the amount they eat, but there are other ingredients from which even a tiny bit can cause life-threatening conditions. In the next section, you will find a more detailed list of the 10 most dangerous food items every dog should avoid.

TOP 10 TOXIC INGREDIENTS TO AVOID

Alcohol – similarly to humans, alcohol–even in small amounts–can damage dogs' brain and liver cells. Most dogs love the taste and smell of beer, so it should be kept out of their reach. The same applies to other alcoholic beverages as well.

Avocado – did you know avocado contains a fungicidal toxin? It's called persin, and while it's not dangerous for humans, it's highly toxic for dogs. Eating too much avocado–leaves, barks, and fruit included–can cause vomiting and diarrhea. The large seed of avocados can also cause issues if swallowed. It can cause blockage in the stomach or the intestines, which can be fatal.

Chocolate – by now, most people know that chocolate is bad for dogs. Do you know why? The main problem is theobromine, an alkaloid of the cacao bean, which is present in all kinds of chocolate. In huge amounts, it can damage the heart and the nervous system. Vomiting, diarrhea, and hyperactivity are the main symptoms of chocolate poisoning.

Coffee & Tea – the caffeine in coffee and tea can be fatal to dogs; even coffee beans can be dangerous. If your dog has caffeine, contact your vet immediately.

Grapes & Raisins – some people say their dog eats all the grapes in the garden without any issues. This is simply good luck and doesn't mean grapes or raisins are good for your pup. On the contrary, they can cause kidney failure, and a small amount can cause continuous vomiting and lethargy.

Macadamia Nuts – the ingestion of these nuts–even in small amounts–can be fatal for dogs. Keep your dog away from macadamia nuts or food that contains these. The most obvious symptoms of macadamia nut poisoning are vomiting, fever, and seizures.

Onions and garlic – all kinds of onions and garlic are highly toxic for dogs. They can **kill red blood cells,** which consequently can lead to anemia. Watch out for food containing powdered onion or garlic, too. Vomiting and breathing difficulties are the first symptoms of onion-poisoning.

Peach pits – peach and plum pits contain cyanide, which is highly toxic for humans and dogs. If dogs eat pits and cyanide is released, it can be fatal in a matter of minutes. The signs to watch out for are excessive salivation, breathing difficulties, paralysis, and rapid heart beat.

Unbaked Yeast Dough – don't let your dog taste your favorite donut–especially the fresh yeast dough. This type of dough rises in warm temperatures, and it's exactly what it does in dogs' stomachs. It stretches the stomach, which can be painful for dogs.

Xylitol or Birch Sugar – artificial sweeteners can cause **liver failure** in dogs in a few days. Some of the symptoms are lethargy, vomiting, coordination issues, and seizures. Try to keep food that is packed with xylitol out of reach of your pup.

FEEDING GUIDELINES & CALORIE CALCULATION

Now let's talk about a very important topic when it comes to preparing food for your dogs. As you can imagine, knowing and choosing the right ingredients and creating balanced mixes is crucial, but it's not enough. It's equally important to know how to prepare the right portions so as not to exceed the calories, neither too much nor too little. Of course, dogs of different life stages, activity levels, and health conditions may require more or less. Puppies have different nutritional needs than adults, as do neutered/spayed dogs or dogs that are nursing, which may require adjustments to their standard feeding conditions that a responsible dog parent should consider.

To determine the Resting Energy Requirements (RER) of your dog, you will need to do some calculations. The formula may seem intimidating at first:

RER = 70*(kg Ideal Body Weight) ^0.75

However, it is not as complicated as it appears. Simply grab a calculator and follow these steps to break down the information into easily understandable chunks.

1. Start by determining the weight of your dog. For instance, let's assume that your dog weighs 30 pounds. To convert this weight into kilograms, you need to divide 30 by 2.2, which will give you 13.64 kg.

2. Take your dog's weight in kilograms to the power of 0.75. This is known as the exponent and is represented by the ^ symbol in the formula. On your calculator, it will look like an x^y symbol. For instance, in this case, the calculation would involve raising 13.64 to the power of 0.75, resulting in 7.09. This is the most difficult part of the formula, but you can easily use a free online scientific calculator.

3. Multiply this number by 70 to get the Resting Energy Requirement (RER). In this instance, the RER would be 496 kcal.

Once you have obtained the RER, it will be easy to calculate your dog's **Daily Energy Requirement (DER).** You simply need to adjust the RER by applying multipliers that depend on your dog's age and activity level. Here is a table inspired by the Veterinary Medical Center of the Ohio State University that contains the most common multipliers that you may need to calculate your dog's actual caloric requirement or DER.

- **Puppy 2-4 months:**   3 x RER
- **Junior 4-12 months:**   2 x RER
- **Neutered adult:**   1.6 x RER (ideal and normal activity)
- **Intact adult:**   1.8 x RER (ideal and normal activity)
- **For overweight dogs:**   1 x RER for ideal weight (not actual weight)
- **For underweight dogs:**   1.5 x RER for ideal weight (not actual weight)
- **Very active / working dogs:** 2-4 x RER

   Here are two examples:

4. Neutered adult dog with ideal healthy weight 10 kg and regular daily activities:
   RER= 70 x (10 kg)0.75 = 394 kcal/day (Basic Resting Energy Requirements)
   Condition: Neutered dog (1.6 x RER)
   DER = 1.6 x 394 = **630 kcal/day**

5. Active Junior dog, healthy weight 5 kg
   RER= 70 x (5 kg)0.75 = 234 kcal/day (Basic Resting Energy Requirements)
   Condition: Junior dog (2 x RER)
   DER = 2 x 234 = **468 kcal/day**

The topic of food portions is not simple at all, individual needs can vary, so these calculations are only starting points to decide on the actual dog's calorie needs, and it's important to remember that determining your own dog's ideal weight and caloric needs should be done with the assistance of your veterinarian to avoid any mistakes. It's always useful to regularly monitor your furry friend's weight to ensure they maintain their ideal weight.

HOMEMADE FOOD PORTION GUIDE

This book, in the recipe section, has been designed to be easy to use regardless of your dog's breed or size, or their caloric and nutritional needs, so that you can transition together from old, highly-processed food to a safe and healthy diet. The aim of this book is to make sure that you have not only well-balanced recipes that provide your dog with all the nutrients they need to be happy, strong, and healthy, but also an accurate method that you can rely on when cooking for them, so that you can portion the right amounts without risking mistakes.

Once you have calculated your dog's Daily Energy Requirement (DER) and verified with your veterinarian that it is correct, you can easily cook and prepare portions for your pet.
All the recipes you will find in this book are balanced, and you will notice that each recipe provides the exact amount of calories contained in 100g of prepared food.
In this way, with a simple proportion, you can create customized portions for your dog based on their specific caloric needs.

Let's take an example:
Dog weight 10 kg
Neutered Adult with Normal Activity
Caloric requirement according to the formula is **634 kcal/day**

Recipe which contains **120 kcal per 100g**
Let's calculate the right portion using this simple formula:
120 kcal : 100 g = 643 kcal : X
Daily portion: 100 x 643 / 41 = **536 g**

The daily portion of this specific meal for this dog will be **536 g**

CHAPTER 3
FREQUENTLY ASKED QUESTIONS

Still have questions? Great! In this section you will find the three most frequently asked questions about homemade dog food. Remember, if you decide to switch to this meal option, you will always learn something new. It's a never-ending learning process which is fun for you, and your "official food taster" will be happy to join you in this adventure.

COOKING FOR YOUR DOG: IS IT COST-EFFECTIVE?

The short answer is YES, it is! When buying ingredients for your pup's meal, you will see how versatile it can be and the good news is, it is cheaper or roughly the same price as processed dog food, but the quality is much, much better. For example, buying in bulk is a great way to cut expenses, and there are many online stores that offer subscription options too.

DOES COOKING FOR YOUR DOG TAKE A LOT OF TIME?

Time is an important factor when it comes to cooking for your dog, and many people say they don't have time to do it every day. However, there are many options to choose from: raw feeding does not require cooking and it's the least time-consuming diet type. But cooking isn't as time-consuming as you might think. Cooking meat does not mean to do so for hours, it's okay to just cook meat until it turns white (longer cooking time is required in case of venison and salmon). Heat treatment is enough to kill unwanted bacteria. Cooking large batches of food and storing it in smaller portions in the freezer is also an option for those who don't want to cook dog food every day.

STORING DOG FOOD: TIPS AND COMMON MISTAKES TO AVOID

Try to find containers that are suitable for freezing. Divide the large batch of food into smaller portions and put them in the fridge (depending on the ingredients, food will stay fresh for 4-5 days in the fridge), or store them in the freezer. Never give spoiled food to your dog.

When handling meat or other ingredients, especially raw food items, one should follow HACCP standards. The ingredients should be bought from reliable sources. Please keep in mind that cooking for your pups is no different than cooking food for humans.

CHAPTER 4
COOKBOOK

SOUP

Yes, dogs can eat soup, too! Veggies and meat-packed soups are great in many ways. They can help to keep your dog hydrated, and if frozen, they can be tasty refreshments during hot summer days. You can boost your dog's food by pouring some soup on it as a topper, and soups can be easily stored in bottles, so they are great to-go water alternatives when you are traveling with your pup. In this section, you'll find soups that are much more than a simple bone broth!

TO MAKE CORRECT PORTIONS:
Every recipe provided in this section is well-balanced, and you will always find the nutritional analysis at the end. However, the most important factor to consider is the calorie intake because based on that, you can easily calculate the correct daily portion for your dog.

Let's take an example: if your dog has a daily energy requirement (DER) of 630 kcal/day and the recipe you are preparing contains 148 kcal per 100 g, you can use this simple formula to determine the appropriate portion:

$$\text{Daily Meal Portion (g)} = 100 \times \text{DER} / \text{Meal kcal}$$

e.g., Daily Meal Portion (g) = 100 x 630 / 148 = 425 g (15 oz)

Remember that **knowing your dog's calorie requirement is essential to help them maintain their ideal weight.** You can use the information found in this book, specifically in the chapter titled "Feeding Guidelines & Calorie Calculation," or seek assistance from a veterinarian for added assurance.

BEEF & BEET SOUP

Ingredients:

- 2 ¾ cup water (650 g)
- 3.5 oz beef (100 g)
- 1.7 oz green tripe (beef) (50 g)
- 5.3 oz beetroot (150 g)
- 1.7 oz apple (50 g)
- 1 tsp rosehip powder (optional)

Nutrition Facts
(Analytical components in 100g):

- Energy   39 kcal
- Fat   3.7 g
- Carbohydrate   2.3 g
- Fiber   0.4 g
- Protein   3.5 g

Preparation:

1. Prepare ingredients at room temperature. Rinse meat carefully.
2. Clean beef and green tripe if necessary (you can leave fatty parts on, or remove half of them).
3. Dice meat and tripe.
4. Cook meat and tripe in water for approximately 15 minutes (amount of water depends on personal preferences) slowly to preserve nutrients.
5. Grate or dice beetroot and apple into tiny cubes.
6. Add beetroot and apple to the mixture, incorporating it carefully.
7. Pour the mixture into a food processor and mix it to get a homogeneous liquid. Alternatively you can use a stick blender.
8. Let the mixture cool down, add rosehip powder if using, then pour into bottles and store in the fridge for 3 days, or freeze it in ice trays/freezer-safe containers.

LAMB & CARROT SOUP

Ingredients:

- 2 ¾ cup water (650 g)
- 5.3 oz lamb (150 g)
- 5.3 oz carrot (150 g)
- 1.7 oz pear (50 g)
- 1 tsp rosehip powder (optional)

Nutrition Facts
(Analytical components in 100g):

- Energy   51 kcal
- Fat   3.1 g
- Carbohydrate   2.1 g
- Fiber   0.7 g
- Protein   3.7 g

Preparation:

1. Prepare ingredients at room temperature. Rinse meat carefully.
2. Clean lamp if necessary (you can leave fatty parts on, or remove half of them).
3. Dice meat into cubes.
4. Cook in water for approximately 15 minutes (amount of water depends on personal preferences) slowly to preserve nutrients.
5. Grate or dice carrot and pear into tiny cubes.
6. Add carrot and pear to the mixture, incorporating it carefully.
7. Pour the mixture into a food processor and mix it to get a homogeneous liquid. Alternatively you can use a stick blender.
8. Let the mixture cool down, add rosehip powder if using, then pour into bottles and store in the fridge for 3 days, or freeze it in ice trays/freezer-safe containers.

CHICKEN & VEGGIE SOUP

Ingredients:

- 2 ¾ cup water (650 g)
- 5.3 oz chicken thighs (150 g)
- 3.5 oz carrot (100 g)
- 1.7 oz pumpkin (baked) (50 g)
- 1.7 oz apple (50 g)
- 1 tsp rosehip powder (optional)

Nutrition Facts
(Analytical components in 100g):

- Energy   41 kcal
- Fat   2.1 g
- Carbohydrate   2 g
- Fiber   0.5 g
- Protein   3.8 g

Preparation:

1. Prepare ingredients at room temperature. Rinse meat carefully. Remove bones from the thighs, leave skin and fat on.
2. Clean thighs carefully if necessary.
3. Cut meat into cubes.
4. Cook meat in water for approximately 15 minutes (amount of water depends on personal preferences) slowly to preserve nutrients.
5. Peel and cut baked pumpkin and carrot into tiny cubes.
6. Add carrot, apple, and pumpkin to the mixture, incorporating it carefully.
7. Pour the mixture into a food processor and mix it to get a homogeneous liquid. You can use a stick blender for mixing.
8. Let the mixture cool down, add rosehip powder if using, then pour into bottles and store in the fridge for 3 days, or freeze it in ice trays or freezer-safe containers.

CHICKEN & PARSNIP SOUP

Ingredients:

- 2 ½ cup water (600 g)
- 7 oz chicken breast (200 g)
- 3.5 oz carrot (100 g)
- 1.7 oz parsnip (50 g)
- 1.7 oz banana (50 g)
- 1 tsp rosehip powder (optional)

Nutrition Facts
(Analytical components in 100g):

- Energy   38 kcal
- Fat   0.6 g
- Carbohydrate   2.6 g
- Fiber   0.7 g
- Protein   5 g

Preparation:

1. Prepare ingredients at room temperature. Rinse meat carefully. Remove bones from the chicken breast, leave skin and fat on.
2. Clean chicken breast carefully if necessary.
3. Cut meat into cubes.
4. Cook meat in water for approximately 15 minutes (amount of water depends on personal preferences) slowly to preserve nutrients.
5. Peel and cut parsnip, banana, and carrot into tiny cubes.
6. Add carrot, parsnip, and banana to the mixture, incorporating it carefully.
7. Pour the mixture into a food processor and mix it to get a homogeneous liquid. You can use a stick blender for mixing.
8. Let the mixture cool down, add rosehip powder if using, then pour into bottles and store in the fridge for 3 days, or freeze it in ice trays or freezer-safe containers.

VEGGIE MIX SOUP

Ingredients:

- 2 ¾ cup water (650 g)
- 3.5 oz beetroot (100 g)
- 1.7 oz pumpkin (50 g)
- 5.3 oz carrot (150 g)
- 1.7 oz zucchini (50 g)
- 1 tsp rosehip powder (optional)

Preparation:

1. Prepare ingredients at room temperature. Rinse veggies carefully.
2. Peel and dice veggies.
3. Cook veggies in water for approximately 15 minutes (amount of water depends on personal preferences) slowly to preserve nutrients.
4. Pour the mixture into a food processor and mix it to get a homogeneous liquid. Alternatively you can use a stick blender.
5. Let the mixture cool down, add rosehip powder if using, then pour into bottles and store in the fridge for 3 days, or freeze it in ice trays/freezer-safe containers.

Nutrition Facts
(Analytical components in 100g):

- Energy   11 kcal
- Fat   0 g
- Carbohydrate   2.9 g
- Fiber   0.9 g
- Protein   0.5 g

LOW-FAT PUPLOAF

In this section you will find simple and quick puploaf recipes that are grain-free, low in fat, and low in carbohydrates. They are perfect for weight management, and you can decide whether to serve them raw or baked. Please keep in mind that if you choose the baked version, you should not add any bones to the food, and you should provide calcium supplementation.

If you decide to try the raw option, simply don't cook the meat. Prepare it ground or cut into small pieces and serve it raw directly in the bowl with the other ingredients. Buy ingredients from reliable sources only and do not use meat from the wild, such as squirrels or venison. **Never feed pork raw.** *Keep in mind that not all dogs enjoy raw meat, especially if they have been accustomed to traditional commercial canned food. In general, this type of feeding requires some patience in the beginning, as your dog may need to get used to it. You can experiment or gradually reduce the cooking time. Remember to pay special attention to kitchen hygiene when handling raw meat. Always clean surfaces and utensils thoroughly to avoid contamination.*

TO MAKE CORRECT PORTIONS:
Every recipe provided in this section is well-balanced, and you will always find the nutritional analysis at the end. However, the most important factor to consider is the calorie intake because based on that, you can easily calculate the correct daily portion for your dog.
Let's take an example: if your dog has a daily energy requirement (DER) of 630 kcal/day and the recipe you are preparing contains 148 kcal per 100 g, you can use this simple formula to determine the appropriate portion:

$$\text{Daily Meal Portion (g)} = 100 \times \text{DER} / \text{Meal kcal}$$

e.g., Daily Meal Portion (g) = 100 x 630 / 148 = 425 g (15 oz)

Remember that **knowing your dog's calorie requirement is essential to help them maintain their ideal weight.** You can use the information found in this book, specifically in the chapter titled "Feeding Guidelines & Calorie Calculation," or seek assistance from a veterinarian for added assurance.

CHICKEN & CARROT

Ingredients:

- 14 oz chicken thighs (400 g)
- 10.6 oz chicken breast (300 g)
- 3.5 oz offal (1 oz chicken liver, 0.7 oz chicken heart, 1.7 chicken gizzard) (100 g)
- 7 oz carrot (200 g)

Nutrition Facts
(Analytical components in 100g):

- Energy   149 kcal
- Fat   6.7 g
- Carbohydrate 2,2 g
- Fiber   0.6 g
- Protein   20.8 g

Preparation:

1. Prepare ingredients at room temperature. Remove all the skin and fat from the thighs and breast. Remove bones if you're going to bake the loaf. Rinse meat carefully.
2. Clean liver, heart, and gizzard thoroughly, soak them in cold water, and remove connective tissues.
3. Cut thighs, breast, offal into cubes and feed them through a meat grinder.
4. Dice carrot into tiny cubes and add it to the mixture.
5. Mix it carefully.
6. Preheat the oven to 356 F (180° C), pour the mixture into a mold and bake for approximately 30 minutes, until golden brown.
7. Let it cool down completely, then serve or freeze in portions.

*You can also try this recipe in the raw meat version.

CHICKEN & SWEET POTATO

Ingredients:

- 14 oz chicken thighs (400 g)
- 10.6 oz chicken breast (300 g)
- 3.5 oz offal (1 oz chicken liver, 0.7 oz chicken heart, 1.7 chicken gizzard) (100 g)
- 7 oz sweet potato (200 g)

Nutrition Facts
(Analytical components in 100g):

- Energy   156 kcal
- Fat   6.9 g
- Carbohydrate 3.8 g
- Fiber   0.6 g
- Protein   21 g

Preparation:

1. Prepare ingredients at room temperature. Remove all the skin and fat from the thighs and breast. Remove bones if you're going to bake the loaf. Rinse meat carefully.
2. Clean liver, heart, and gizzard thoroughly, soak them in cold water, and remove connective tissues.
3. Cut thighs, breast, offal into cubes and feed them through a meat grinder.
4. Dice sweet potato into tiny cubes and add it to the mixture.
5. Mix it carefully.
6. Preheat the oven to 356 F (180° C), pour the mixture into a mold and bake for approximately 30 minutes, until golden brown.
7. Let it cool down completely, then serve or freeze in portions.

*You can also try this recipe in the raw meat version.

CHICKEN & PUMPKIN

Ingredients:

- 14 oz chicken thighs (400 g)
- 10.6 oz chicken breast (300 g)
- 3.5 oz offal (1 oz chicken liver, 0.7 oz chicken heart, 1.7 chicken gizzard) (100 g)
- 7 oz pumpkin (200 g)

Nutrition Facts
(Analytical components in 100g):

- Energy   144 kcal
- Fat   6.9 g
- Carbohydrate   1 g
- Fiber   0.2 g
- Protein   20.7 g

Preparation:

1. Prepare ingredients at room temperature. Remove all the skin and fat from the thighs and breast. Remove bones if you're going to bake the loaf. Rinse meat carefully.
2. Clean liver, heart, and gizzard thoroughly, soak them in cold water, and remove connective tissues.
3. Cut thighs, breast, offal into cubes and feed them through a meat grinder.
4. Dice pumpkin into tiny cubes and add it to the mixture. You can use unsweetened pumpkin puree, too.
5. Mix it carefully.
6. Preheat the oven to 356 F (180° C), pour the mixture into a mold and bake for approximately 30 minutes, until golden brown.
7. Let it cool down completely, then serve or freeze in portions.

*You can also try this recipe in the raw meat version.

CHICKEN & BEETROOT

Ingredients:

- 14 oz chicken thighs (400 g)
- 10.6 oz chicken breast (300 g)
- 3.5 oz offal (1 oz chicken liver, 0.7 oz chicken heart, 1.7 chicken gizzard) (100 g)
- 7 oz beetroot (200 g)

Nutrition Facts
(Analytical components in 100g):

- Energy   148 kcal
- Fat   6.9 g
- Carbohydrate   2 g
- Fiber   0.4 g
- Protein   21 g

Preparation:

1. Prepare ingredients at room temperature. Remove all the skin and fat from the thighs and breast. Remove bones if you're going to bake the loaf. Rinse meat carefully.
2. Clean liver, heart, and gizzard thoroughly, soak them in cold water, and remove connective tissues.
3. Cut thighs, breast, offal into cubes and feed them through a meat grinder.
4. Dice beetroot into tiny cubes and add it to the mixture. It's easier if you pre-cook beetroot.
5. Mix it carefully.
6. Preheat the oven to 356 F (180° C), pour the mixture into a mold and bake for approximately 30 minutes, until golden brown.
7. Let it cool down completely, then serve or freeze in portions.

*You can also try this recipe in the raw meat version.

CHICKEN & VEGGIE MIX 1

Ingredients:

- 14 oz chicken thighs (400 g)
- 10.6 oz chicken breast (300 g)
- 3.5 oz offal (1 oz chicken liver, 0.7 oz chicken heart, 1.7 chicken gizzard) (100 g)
- 3.5 oz carrot (100 g)
- 3.5 oz pumpkin (100 g)

Nutrition Facts
(Analytical components in 100g):

- Energy   146 kcal
- Fat   6.9 g
- Carbohydrate   1.6 g
- Fiber   0.4 g
- Protein   20.8 g

Preparation:

1. Prepare ingredients at room temperature. Remove all the skin and fat from the thighs and breast. Remove bones if you're going to bake the loaf. Rinse meat carefully.
2. Clean liver, heart, and gizzard thoroughly, soak them in cold water, and remove connective tissues.
3. Cut thighs, breast, offal into cubes and feed them through a meat grinder.
4. Dice carrot and pumpkin into tiny cubes and add it to the mixture.
5. Mix it carefully.
6. Preheat the oven to 356 F (180° C), pour the mixture into a mold and bake for approximately 30 minutes, until golden brown.
7. Let it cool down completely, then serve or freeze in portions.

*You can also try this recipe in the raw meat version.

CHICKEN & VEGGIE MIX 2

Ingredients:

- 14 oz chicken thighs (400 g)
- 10.6 oz chicken breast (300 g)
- 3.5 oz offal (1 oz chicken liver, 0.7 oz chicken heart, 1.7 chicken gizzard) (100 g)
- 3.5 oz carrot (100 g)
- 3.5 oz sweet potato (100 g)

Nutrition Facts
(Analytical components in 100g):

- Energy   153 kcal
- Fat   6.9 g
- Carbohydrate   3 g
- Fiber   0.6 g
- Protein   20.8 g

Preparation:

1. Prepare ingredients at room temperature. Remove all the skin and fat from the thighs and breast. Remove bones if you're going to bake the loaf. Rinse meat carefully.
2. Clean liver, heart, and gizzard thoroughly, soak them in cold water, and remove connective tissues.
3. Cut thighs, breast, offal into cubes and feed them through a meat grinder.
4. Dice carrot and sweet potato into tiny cubes and add it to the mixture.
5. Mix it carefully.
6. Preheat the oven to 356 F (180° C), pour the mixture into a mold and bake for approximately 30 minutes, until golden brown.
7. Let it cool down completely, then serve or freeze in portions.

*You can also try this recipe in the raw meat version.

CHICKEN & VEGGIE MIX 3

Ingredients:

- 14 oz chicken thighs (400 g)
- 10.6 oz chicken breast (300 g)
- 3.5 oz offal (1 oz chicken liver, 0.7 oz chicken heart, 1.7 chicken gizzard) (100 g)
- 3.5 oz carrot (100 g)
- 3.5 oz broccoli (100 g)

Nutrition Facts
(Analytical components in 100g):

- Energy   149 kcal
- Fat   6.9 g
- Carbohydrate 1.7 g
- Fiber   0.5 g
- Protein   20.8 g

Preparation:

1. Prepare ingredients at room temperature. Remove all the skin and fat from the thighs and breast. Remove bones if you're going to bake the loaf. Rinse meat carefully.
2. Clean liver, heart, and gizzard thoroughly, soak them in cold water, and remove connective tissues.
3. Cut thighs, breast, offal into cubes and feed them through a meat grinder.
4. Dice carrot and broccoli into tiny cubes and add it to the mixture.
5. Mix it carefully.
6. Preheat the oven to 356 F (180° C), pour the mixture into a mold and bake for approximately 30 minutes, until golden brown.
7. Let it cool down completely, then serve or freeze in portions.

*You can also try this recipe in the raw meat version.

CHICKEN & VEGGIE MIX 4

Ingredients:

- 14 oz chicken thighs (400 g)
- 10.6 oz chicken breast (300 g)
- 3.5 oz offal (1 oz chicken liver, 0.7 oz chicken heart, 1.7 chicken gizzard) (100 g)
- 3.5 oz carrot (100 g)
- 3.5 oz beetroot (100 g)

Nutrition Facts
(Analytical components in 100g):

- Energy   149 kcal
- Fat   6.9 g
- Carbohydrate 1.3 g
- Fiber   0.5 g
- Protein   20.7 g

Preparation:

1. Prepare ingredients at room temperature. Remove all the skin and fat from the thighs and breast. Remove bones if you're going to bake the loaf. Rinse meat carefully.
2. Clean liver, heart, and gizzard thoroughly, soak them in cold water, and remove connective tissues.
3. Cut thighs, breast, offal into cubes and feed them through a meat grinder.
4. Dice carrot and beetroot into tiny cubes and add it to the mixture. It's easier if you pre-cook beetroot.
5. Mix it carefully.
6. Preheat the oven to 356 F (180° C), pour the mixture into a mold and bake for approximately 30 minutes, until golden brown.
7. Let it cool down completely, then serve or freeze in portions.

*You can also try this recipe in the raw meat version.

CHICKEN & BLUEBERRY

Ingredients:

- 14 oz chicken thighs (400 g)
- 10.6 oz chicken breast (300 g)
- 3.5 oz offal (1 oz chicken liver, 0.7 oz chicken heart, 1.7 chicken gizzard) (100 g)
- 5.3 oz carrot (150 g)
- 31.7 oz blueberries (50 g)

Nutrition Facts
(Analytical components in 100g):

- Energy   148 kcal
- Fat   6.9 g
- Carbohydrate   2.1 g
- Fiber   1.4 g
- Protein   20.7 g

Preparation:

1. Prepare ingredients at room temperature. Remove all the skin and fat from the thighs and breast. Remove bones if you're going to bake the loaf. Rinse meat carefully.
2. Clean liver, heart, and gizzard thoroughly, soak them in cold water, and remove connective tissues.
3. Cut thighs, breast, offal into cubes and feed them through a meat grinder.
4. Dice carrot into tiny cubes and add it to the mixture. Add blueberries.
5. Mix it carefully.
6. Preheat the oven to 356 F (180° C), pour the mixture into a mold and bake for approximately 30 minutes, until golden brown.
7. Let it cool down completely, then serve or freeze in portions.

*You can also try this recipe in the raw meat version.

SUPER LEAN CHICKEN & CARROT

Ingredients:

- 24.7 oz chicken breast (700 g)
- 3.5 oz offal (1 oz chicken liver, 0.7 oz chicken heart, 1.7 chicken gizzard) (100 g)
- 7 oz carrot (200 g)

Nutrition Facts
(Analytical components in 100g):

- Energy   143 kcal
- Fat   3 g
- Carbohydrate   2.2 g
- Fiber   0.6 g
- Protein   25.7 g

Preparation:

1. Prepare ingredients at room temperature. Remove all the skin and fat from the breast. Remove bones if you're going to bake the loaf. Rinse meat carefully.
2. Clean liver, heart, and gizzard thoroughly, soak them in cold water, and remove connective tissues.
3. Cut breast and offal into cubes and feed them through a meat grinder.
4. Dice carrot into tiny cubes and add it to the mixture.
5. Mix it carefully.
6. Preheat the oven to 356 F (180° C), pour the mixture into a mold and bake for approximately 30 minutes, until golden brown.
7. Let it cool down completely, then serve or freeze in portions.

*You can also try this recipe in the raw meat version.

DUCK & CARROT

Ingredients:

- 24.7 oz duck (700 g)
- 3.5 oz offal (1 oz chicken liver, 0.7 oz chicken heart, 1.7 chicken gizzard) (100 g)
- 7 oz carrot (200 g)

Nutrition Facts
(Analytical components in 100g):

- Energy   262 kcal
- Fat   15.6 g
- Carbohydrate   2.2 g
- Fiber   0.6 g
- Protein   17 g

Preparation:

1. Prepare ingredients at room temperature. Remove all the skin and fat from the meat. Remove bones if you're going to bake the loaf. Rinse meat carefully.
2. Clean liver, heart, and gizzard thoroughly, soak them in cold water, and remove connective tissues.
3. Cut meat and offal into cubes and feed them through a meat grinder.
4. Dice carrot into tiny cubes and add it to the mixture.
5. Mix it carefully.
6. Preheat the oven to 356 F (180° C), pour the mixture into a mold and bake for approximately 30 minutes, until golden brown.
7. Let it cool down completely, then serve or freeze in portions.

*You can also try this recipe in the raw meat version.

DUCK & CHICKEN

Ingredients:

- 14 oz duck (400 g)
- 10.6 oz chicken breast (300 g)
- 3.5 oz offal (1 oz chicken liver, 0.7 oz chicken heart, 1.7 chicken gizzard) (100 g)
- 7 oz carrot (200 g)

Nutrition Facts
(Analytical components in 100g):

- Energy   179 kcal
- Fat   8.5 g
- Carbohydrate   2.2 g
- Fiber   0.6 g
- Protein   18.5 g

Preparation:

1. Prepare ingredients at room temperature. Remove all the skin and fat from the meat. Remove bones if you're going to bake the loaf. Rinse meat carefully.
2. Clean liver, heart, and gizzard thoroughly, soak them in cold water, and remove connective tissues.
3. Cut meat and offal into cubes and feed them through a meat grinder.
4. Dice carrot into tiny cubes and add it to the mixture.
5. Mix it carefully.
6. Preheat the oven to 356 F (180° C), pour the mixture into a mold and bake for approximately 30 minutes, until golden brown.
7. Let it cool down completely, then serve or freeze in portions.

*You can also try this recipe in the raw meat version.

DUCK & VEGGIE MIX

Ingredients:

- 24.7 oz duck (700 g)
- 3.5 oz offal (1 oz chicken liver, 0.7 oz chicken heart, 1.7 chicken gizzard) (100 g)
- 3.5 oz pumpkin (100 g)
- 3.5 oz sweet potato (100 g)

Nutrition Facts
(Analytical components in 100g):

- Energy   335 kcal
- Fat   15 g
- Carbohydrate   2.4 g
- Fiber   0.4 g
- Protein   16.6 g

Preparation:

1. Prepare ingredients at room temperature. Remove all the skin and fat from the meat. Remove bones if you're going to bake the loaf. Rinse meat carefully.
2. Clean liver, heart, and gizzard thoroughly, soak them in cold water, and remove connective tissues.
3. Cut meat and offal into cubes and feed them through a meat grinder.
4. Dice pumpkin and sweet potato into tiny cubes and add it to the mixture.
5. Mix it carefully.
6. Preheat the oven to 356 F (180° C), pour the mixture into a mold and bake for approximately 30 minutes, until golden brown.
7. Let it cool down completely, then serve or freeze in portions.

*You can also try this recipe in the raw meat version.

BEEF, TRIPE & CARROT

Ingredients:

- 21.2 oz beef (lean) (600 g)
- 3.5 oz offal (1 oz chicken liver, 0.7 oz chicken heart, 1.7 chicken gizzard) (100 g)
- 5.3 oz beef green tripe (150 g)
- 5.3 oz carrot (150 g)

Nutrition Facts
(Analytical components in 100g):

- Energy   165 kcal
- Fat   7.8 g
- Carbohydrate   2.3 g
- Fiber   0.1 g
- Protein   21.3 g

Preparation:

1. Prepare ingredients at room temperature. Remove any fat from the meat. Remove bones if you're going to bake the loaf. Rinse meat carefully.
2. Clean the liver thoroughly, soak in cold water and remove connective tissues.
3. Cut meat, green tripe and offal into cubes and feed them through a meat grinder.
4. Dice carrot into tiny cubes and add it to the mixture.
5. Mix it carefully.
6. Preheat the oven to 356 F (180° C), pour the mixture into a mold and bake for approximately 30 minutes, until golden brown.
7. Let it cool down completely, then serve or freeze in portions.

*You can also try this recipe in the raw meat version.

BEEF, TRIPE & SWEET POTATO

Ingredients:

- 21.2 oz beef (lean) (600g)
- 3.5 oz offal (1.7 oz beef liver, 1.7 oz beef heart) (100 g)
- 5.3 oz beef green tripe (150 g)
- 5.3 oz sweet potato (150 g)

Nutrition Facts
(Analytical components in 100g):

- Energy   170 kcal
- Fat   7.8 g
- Carbohydrate   3.1 g
- Fiber   0.4 g
- Protein   21.1 g

Preparation:

1. Prepare ingredients at room temperature. Remove any fat from the meat. Remove bones if you're going to bake the loaf. Rinse meat carefully.
2. Clean the liver thoroughly, soak in cold water, and remove connective tissues.
3. Cut meat, green tripe, and offal into cubes and feed them through a meat grinder.
4. Dice sweet potato into tiny cubes and add it to the mixture.
5. Mix it carefully.
6. Preheat the oven to 356 F (180° C), pour the mixture into a mold and bake for approximately 30 minutes, until golden brown.
7. Let it cool down completely, then serve or freeze in portions.

*You can also try this recipe in the raw meat version.

BEEF, TRIPE & PUMPKIN

Ingredients:

- 21.2 oz beef (lean) (600 g)
- 3.5 oz offal (1.7 oz beef liver, 1.7 oz beef heart) (100 g)
- 5.3 oz beef green tripe (150g)
- 5.3 oz pumpkin (150g)

Nutrition Facts
(Analytical components in 100g):

- Energy   164 kcal
- Fat   7.8 g
- Carbohydrate   1.7 g
- Fiber   0.2 g
- Protein   21 g

Preparation:

1. Prepare ingredients at room temperature. Remove any fat from the meat. Remove bones if you're going to bake the loaf. Rinse meat carefully.
2. Clean the liver thoroughly, soak in cold water, and remove connective tissues.
3. Cut meat, green tripe, and offal into cubes and feed them through a meat grinder.
4. Dice pumpkin into tiny cubes and add it to the mixture.
5. Mix it carefully.
6. Preheat the oven to 356 F (180° C), pour the mixture into a mold and bake for approximately 30 minutes, until golden brown.
7. Let it cool down completely, then serve or freeze in portions.

*You can also try this recipe in the raw meat version.

BEEF, TRIPE & BEETROOT

Ingredients:

- 21.2 oz beef (lean) (600 g)
- 3.5 oz offal (1.7 oz beef liver, 1.7 oz beef heart) (100 g)
- 5.3 oz beef green tripe (150 g)
- 5.3 oz beetroot (150 g)

Nutrition Facts
(Analytical components in 100g):

- Energy   165 kcal
- Fat   7.8 g
- Carbohydrate   2 g
- Fiber   0.4 g
- Protein   21 g

Preparation:

1. Prepare ingredients at room temperature. Remove any fat from the meat. Remove bones if you're going to bake the loaf. Rinse meat carefully.
2. Clean the liver thoroughly, soak in cold water, and remove connective tissues.
3. Cut meat, green tripe, and offal into cubes and feed them through a meat grinder.
4. Dice beetroot into tiny cubes and add it to the mixture. It's easier if you pre-cook beetroot.
5. Mix it carefully.
6. Preheat the oven to 356 F (180° C), pour the mixture into a mold and bake for approximately 30 minutes, until golden brown.
7. Let it cool down completely, then serve or freeze in portions.

*You can also try this recipe in the raw meat version.

BEEF, TRIPE & VEGGIE MIX 1

Ingredients:

- 21.2 oz beef (lean) (600 g)
- 3.5 oz offal (1.7 oz beef liver, 1.7 oz beef heart) (100 g)
- 5.3 oz beef green tripe (150 g)
- 3.5 oz carrot (100 g)
- 1.7 oz sweet potato (50 g)

Nutrition Facts
(Analytical components in 100g):

- Energy   168 kcal
- Fat   7.8 g
- Carbohydrate   2.2 g
- Fiber   0.4 g
- Protein   20.9 g

Preparation:

1. Prepare ingredients at room temperature. Remove any fat from the meat. Remove bones if you're going to bake the loaf. Rinse meat carefully.
2. Clean the liver thoroughly, soak in cold water, and remove connective tissues.
3. Cut meat, green tripe, and offal into cubes and feed them through a meat grinder.
4. Dice carrot and sweet potato into tiny cubes and add it to the mixture.
5. Mix it carefully.
6. Preheat the oven to 356 F (180° C), pour the mixture into a mold and bake for approximately 30 minutes, until golden brown.
7. Let it cool down completely, then serve or freeze in portions.

*You can also try this recipe in the raw meat version.

BEEF, TRIPE & VEGGIE MIX 2

Ingredients:

- 21.2 oz beef (lean) (600 g)
- 3.5 oz offal (1.7 oz beef liver, 1.7 oz beef heart) (100 g)
- 5.3 oz beef green tripe (150 g)
- 3.5 oz sweet potato (100 g)
- 1.7 oz beetroot (50 g)

Nutrition Facts
(Analytical components in 100g):

- Energy   201 kcal
- Fat   9 g
- Carbohydrate   2.9 g
- Fiber   0.4 g
- Protein   20.3 g

Preparation:

1. Prepare ingredients at room temperature. Remove any fat from the meat. Remove bones if you're going to bake the loaf. Rinse meat carefully.
2. Clean the liver thoroughly, soak in cold water, and remove connective tissues.
3. Cut meat, green tripe, and offal into cubes and feed them through a meat grinder.
4. Dice sweet potato and beetroot into tiny cubes and add it to the mixture. It's easier if you pre-cook beetroot.
5. Mix it carefully.
6. Preheat the oven to 356 F (180° C), pour the mixture into a mold and bake for approximately 30 minutes, until golden brown.
7. Let it cool down completely, then serve or freeze in portions.

*You can also try this recipe in the raw meat version.

BEEF & CARROT

Ingredients:

- 24.7 oz beef (lean) (700 g)
- 3.5 oz offal (1.7 oz beef liver, 1.7 oz beef heart) (100 g)
- 7 oz carrot (200 g)

Nutrition Facts
(Analytical components in 100g):

- Energy   158 kcal
- Fat   8.2 g
- Carbohydrate   2.9 g
- Fiber   0.6 g
- Protein   21.2 g

Preparation:

1. Prepare ingredients at room temperature. Remove any fat from the meat. Remove bones if you're going to bake the loaf. Rinse meat carefully.
2. Clean the liver thoroughly, soak in cold water, and remove connective tissues.
3. Cut meat and offal into cubes and feed them through a meat grinder.
4. Dice carrot into tiny cubes and add it to the mixture.
5. Mix it carefully.
6. Preheat the oven to 356 F (180° C), pour the mixture into a mold and bake for approximately 30 minutes, until golden brown.
7. Let it cool down completely, then serve or freeze in portions.

*You can also try this recipe in the raw meat version.

BEEF & SWEET POTATO

Ingredients:

- 24.7 oz beef (lean) (700 g)
- 3.5 oz offal (1.7 oz beef liver, 1.7 oz beef heart) (100 g)
- 7 oz sweet potato (200 g)

Nutrition Facts
(Analytical components in 100g):

- Energy   165 kcal
- Fat   8.2 g
- Carbohydrate   4.5 g
- Fiber   0.6 g
- Protein   21.4 g

Preparation:

1. Prepare ingredients at room temperature. Remove any fat from the meat. Remove bones if you're going to bake the loaf. Rinse meat carefully.
2. Clean the liver thoroughly, soak in cold water, and remove connective tissues.
3. Cut meat and offal into cubes and feed them through a meat grinder.
4. Dice sweet potato into tiny cubes and add it to the mixture.
5. Mix it carefully.
6. Preheat the oven to 356 F (180° C), pour the mixture into a mold and bake for approximately 30 minutes, until golden brown.
7. Let it cool down completely, then serve or freeze in portions.

*You can also try this recipe in the raw meat version.

LAMB & CARROT

Ingredients:

- 24.7 oz lamb (lean) (700 g)
- 3.5 oz offal (1.7 oz beef liver, 1.7 oz beef heart) (100 g)
- 7 oz carrot (200 g)

Nutrition Facts
(Analytical components in 100g):

- Energy   158 kcal
- Fat   8.2 g
- Carbohydrate   2.9 g
- Fiber   0.6 g
- Protein   21.2 g

Preparation:

1. Prepare ingredients at room temperature. Remove any fat from the meat. Remove bones if you're going to bake the loaf. Rinse meat carefully.
2. Clean the liver thoroughly, soak in cold water, and remove connective tissues.
3. Cut meat and offal into cubes and feed them through a meat grinder.
4. Dice carrot into tiny cubes and add it to the mixture.
5. Mix it carefully.
6. Preheat the oven to 356 F (180° C), pour the mixture into a mold and bake for approximately 30 minutes, until golden brown.
7. Let it cool down completely, then serve or freeze in portions.

*You can also try this recipe in the raw meat version.

LAMB & SWEET POTATO

Ingredients:

- 24.7 oz lamb (700 g)
- 3.5 oz offal (1.7 oz lamb liver, 1.7 oz lamb heart) (100 g)
- 7 oz sweet potato (200 g)

Nutrition Facts
(Analytical components in 100g):

- Energy   165 kcal
- Fat   8.2 g
- Carbohydrate   4.5 g
- Fiber   0.6 g
- Protein   21.4 g

Preparation:

1. Prepare ingredients at room temperature. Remove any fat from the meat. Remove bones if you're going to bake the loaf. Rinse meat carefully.
2. Clean the liver thoroughly, soak in cold water, and remove connective tissues.
3. Cut meat and offal into cubes and feed them through a meat grinder.
4. Dice sweet potato into tiny cubes and add it to the mixture.
5. Mix it carefully.
6. Preheat the oven to 356 F (180° C), pour the mixture into a mold and bake for approximately 30 minutes, until golden brown.
7. Let it cool down completely, then serve or freeze in portions.

*You can also try this recipe in the raw meat version.

CHICKEN & BEEF

Ingredients:

- 10.6 oz chicken breast (300 g)
- 10.6 oz beef (lean) (300 g)
- 3.5 oz offal (1.7 oz beef liver, 1.7 oz beef heart) (100 g)
- 5.3 oz beef green tripe (150 g)
- 3.5 oz pumpkin (100 g)
- 1.7 oz beetroot (50 g)

Nutrition Facts
(Analytical components in 100g):

- Energy   139 kcal
- Fat   5.2 g
- Carbohydrate   1.7 g
- Fiber   0.1 g
- Protein   18.9 g

Preparation:

1. Prepare ingredients at room temperature. Remove any fat from the meat. Remove bones if you're going to bake the loaf. Rinse meat carefully.
2. Clean the liver thoroughly, soak in cold water, and remove connective tissues.
3. Cut meat, green tripe, and offal into cubes and feed them through a meat grinder.
4. Dice pumpkin and beetroot into tiny cubes and add it to the mixture.
5. Mix it carefully.
6. Preheat the oven to 356 F (180° C), pour the mixture into a mold and bake for approximately 30 minutes, until golden brown.
7. Let it cool down completely, then serve or freeze in portions.

*You can also try this recipe in the raw meat version.

CHICKEN, LAMB & BEEF

Ingredients:

- 10.6 oz chicken breast (300 g)
- 10.6 oz lamb (300 g)
- 3.5 oz offal (1.7 oz beef liver, 1.7 oz beef heart) (100 g)
- 5.3 oz beef green tripe (150 g)
- 3.5 oz carrot (100 g)
- 1.7 oz beetroot (50 g)

Nutrition Facts
(Analytical components in 100g):

- Energy   170 kcal
- Fat   8.7 g
- Carbohydrate   2.3 g
- Fiber   0.3 g
- Protein   19.1 g

Preparation:

1. Prepare ingredients at room temperature. Remove any fat from the meat. Remove bones if you're going to bake the loaf. Rinse meat carefully.
2. Clean the liver thoroughly, soak in cold water, and remove connective tissues.
3. Cut meat, green tripe, and offal into cubes and feed them through a meat grinder.
4. Dice carrot and beetroot into tiny cubes and add it to the mixture.
5. Mix it carefully.
6. Preheat the oven to 356 F (180° C), pour the mixture into a mold and bake for approximately 30 minutes, until golden brown.
7. Let it cool down completely, then serve or freeze in portions.

*You can also try this recipe in the raw meat version.

CHICKEN & KANGAROO

Ingredients:

- 14 oz chicken breast (400 g)
- 12.3 oz kangaroo (350 g)
- 3.5 oz offal (1.1 oz chicken liver, 0.7 oz chicken heart) (100 g)
- 3.5 oz carrot (100 g)
- 1.7 oz blueberries (50 g)

Nutrition Facts
(Analytical components in 100g):

- Energy   142 kcal
- Fat   3.3 g
- Carbohydrate   1.9 g
- Fiber   0.4 g
- Protein   24.8 g

Preparation:

1. Prepare ingredients at room temperature. Remove all the skin and fat from the meat. Remove bones if you're going to bake the loaf. Rinse meat carefully.
2. Clean the liver thoroughly, soak in cold water, and remove connective tissues.
3. Cut meat and offal into cubes and feed them through a meat grinder.
4. Dice carrot into tiny cubes and add it to the mixture. Add blueberries.
5. Mix it carefully.
6. Preheat the oven to 356 F (180° C), pour the mixture into a mold and bake for approximately 30 minutes, until golden brown.
7. Let it cool down completely, then serve or freeze in portions.

*You can also try this recipe in the raw meat version.

BEEF & KANGAROO

Ingredients:

- 14 oz beef (lean) (400 g)
- 12.3 oz kangaroo (350 g)
- 3.5 oz offal (1.7 oz beef liver, 1.7 oz beef heart) (100 g)
- 3.5 oz carrot (100 g)
- 1.7 oz blueberries (50 g)

Nutrition Facts
(Analytical components in 100g):

- Energy   168 kcal
- Fat   6.8 g
- Carbohydrate   2.6 g
- Fiber   0.4 g
- Protein   23.5 g

Preparation:

1. Prepare ingredients at room temperature. Remove any fat from the meat. Remove bones if you're going to bake the loaf. Rinse meat carefully.
2. Clean the liver thoroughly, soak in cold water, and remove connective tissues.
3. Cut meat and offal into cubes and feed them through a meat grinder.
4. Dice carrot into tiny cubes and add it to the mixture. Add blueberries.
5. Mix it carefully.
6. Preheat the oven to 356 F (180° C), pour the mixture into a mold and bake for approximately 30 minutes, until golden brown.
7. Let it cool down completely, then serve or freeze in portions.

*You can also try this recipe in the raw meat version.

SUPER LEAN KANGAROO & CARROT

Ingredients:

- 24.7 oz kangaroo (700 g)
- 3.5 oz offal (1.1 oz g chicken liver, 0.7 oz chicken heart, 1.7 oz chicken gizzard) (100 g)
- 7 oz carrot (200 g)

Nutrition Facts
(Analytical components in 100g):

- Energy   126 kcal
- Fat   3.4 g
- Carbohydrate   2.2 g
- Fiber   0.6 g
- Protein   21.1 g

Preparation:

1. Prepare ingredients at room temperature. Remove any fat from the meat. Remove bones if you're going to bake the loaf. Rinse meat carefully.
2. Clean liver, heart, and gizzard thoroughly, soak them in cold water, and remove connective tissues.
3. Cut meat and offal into cubes and feed them through a meat grinder.
4. Dice carrot into tiny cubes and add it to the mixture.
5. Mix it carefully.
6. Preheat the oven to 356 F (180° C), pour the mixture into a mold and bake for approximately 30 minutes, until golden brown.
7. Let it cool down completely, then serve or freeze in portions.

*You can also try this recipe in the raw meat version.

SUPER LEAN KANGAROO & SWEET POTATO

Ingredients:

- 24.7 oz kangaroo (700 g)
- 3.5 oz offal (1.1 oz g chicken liver, 0.7 oz chicken heart, 1.7 oz chicken gizzard) (100 g)
- 7 oz sweet potato (200 g)

Nutrition Facts
(Analytical components in 100g):

- Energy   133 kcal
- Fat   3.4 g
- Carbohydrate 3.8 g
- Fiber   0.6 g
- Protein   21.3 g

Preparation:

1. Prepare ingredients at room temperature. Remove any fat from the meat. Remove bones if you're going to bake the loaf. Rinse meat carefully.
2. Clean liver, heart, and gizzard thoroughly, soak them in cold water, and remove connective tissues.
3. Cut meat and offal into cubes and feed them through a meat grinder.
4. Dice sweet potato into tiny cubes and add it to the mixture.
5. Mix it carefully.
6. Preheat the oven to 356 F (180° C), pour the mixture into a mold and bake for approximately 30 minutes, until golden brown.
7. Let it cool down completely, then serve or freeze in portions.

*You can also try this recipe in the raw meat version.

TURKEY & APPLE

Ingredients:

- 24.7 oz turkey breast (700 g)
- 3.5 oz offal (1.1 oz g chicken liver, 0.7 oz chicken heart, 1.7 oz chicken gizzard) (100 g)
- 3.5 oz carrot (100 g)
- 3.5 oz apple (100 g)

Nutrition Facts
(Analytical components in 100g):

- Energy   108 kcal
- Fat   2.3 g
- Carbohydrate 2.5 g
- Fiber   0.5 g
- Protein   20.1 g

Preparation:

1. Prepare ingredients at room temperature. Remove all the skin and fat from the meat. Remove bones if you're going to bake the loaf. Rinse meat carefully.
2. Clean liver, heart, and gizzard thoroughly, soak them in cold water, and remove connective tissues.
3. Cut meat and offal into cubes and feed them through a meat grinder.
4. Dice carrot and apple into tiny cubes and add it to the mixture.
5. Mix it carefully.
6. Preheat the oven to 356 F (180° C), pour the mixture into a mold and bake for approximately 30 minutes, until golden brown.
7. Let it cool down completely, then serve or freeze in portions.

*You can also try this recipe in the raw meat version.

RABBIT & CARROT

Ingredients:

- 24.7 oz rabbit (700 g)
- 3.5 oz offal (1.1 oz g chicken liver, 0.7 oz chicken heart, 1.7 oz chicken gizzard) (100 g)
- 7 oz carrot (200 g)

Preparation:

1. Prepare ingredients at room temperature. Remove any fat from the meat. Remove bones if you're going to bake the loaf. Rinse meat carefully.
2. Clean liver, heart, and gizzard thoroughly, soak them in cold water, and remove connective tissues.
3. Cut meat and offal into cubes and feed them through a meat grinder.
4. Dice carrot into tiny cubes and add it to the mixture.
5. Mix it carefully.
6. Preheat the oven to 356 F (180° C), pour the mixture into a mold and bake for approximately 30 minutes, until golden brown.
7. Let it cool down completely, then serve or freeze in portions.

*You can also try this recipe in the raw meat version.

Nutrition Facts
(Analytical components in 100g):

- Energy   171 kcal
- Fat   6.5 g
- Carbohydrate 2.2 g
- Fiber   0.6 g
- Protein   25.2 g

RABBIT & PUMPKIN

Ingredients:

- 24.7 oz rabbit (700 g)
- 3.5 oz offal (1.1 oz g chicken liver, 0.7 oz chicken heart, 1.7 oz chicken gizzard) (100 g)
- 7 oz pumpkin (200 g)

Preparation:

1. Prepare ingredients at room temperature. Remove any fat from the meat. Remove bones if you're going to bake the loaf. Rinse meat carefully.
2. Clean liver, heart, and gizzard thoroughly, soak them in cold water, and remove connective tissues.
3. Cut meat and offal into cubes and feed them through a meat grinder.
4. Dice pumpkin into tiny cubes and add it to the mixture.
5. Mix it carefully.
6. Preheat the oven to 356 F (180° C), pour the mixture into a mold and bake for approximately 30 minutes, until golden brown.
7. Let it cool down completely, then serve or freeze in portions.

*You can also try this recipe in the raw meat version.

Nutrition Facts
(Analytical components in 100g):

- Energy   166 kcal
- Fat   6.5 g
- Carbohydrate 1 g
- Fiber   0.2 g
- Protein   25.1 g

RABBIT & CHICKEN

Ingredients:

- 14 oz rabbit (400 g)
- 10.6 oz chicken breast (300 g)
- 3.5 oz offal (1.1 oz g chicken liver, 0.7 oz chicken heart, 1.7 oz chicken gizzard) (100 g)
- 7 oz carrot (200 g)

Nutrition Facts
(Analytical components in 100g):

- Energy   148 kcal
- Fat   4.6 g
- Carbohydrate 2.2 g
- Fiber   0.6 g
- Protein   21.6 g

Preparation:

1. Prepare ingredients at room temperature. Remove all the skin and fat from the meat. Remove bones if you're going to bake the loaf. Rinse meat carefully.
2. Clean liver, heart, and gizzard thoroughly, soak them in cold water and remove connective tissues.
3. Cut meat and offal into cubes and feed them through a meat grinder.
4. Dice carrot into tiny cubes and add it to the mixture.
5. Mix it carefully.
6. Preheat the oven to 356 F (180° C), pour the mixture into a mold and bake for approximately 30 minutes, until golden brown.
7. Let it cool down completely, then serve or freeze in portions.

*You can also try this recipe in the raw meat version.

RABBIT & APPLE

Ingredients:

- 24.7 oz rabbit (700 g)
- 3.5 oz offal (1.1 oz g chicken liver, 0.7 oz chicken heart, 1.7 oz chicken gizzard) (100 g)
- 7 oz apple (200 g)

Nutrition Facts
(Analytical components in 100g):

- Energy   171 kcal
- Fat   6.5 g
- Carbohydrate 2.8 g
- Fiber   0.4 g
- Protein   25 g

Preparation:

1. Prepare ingredients at room temperature. Remove any fat from the meat. Remove bones if you're going to bake the loaf. Rinse meat carefully.
2. Clean liver, heart, and gizzard thoroughly, soak them in cold water, and remove connective tissues.
3. Cut meat and offal into cubes and feed them through a meat grinder.
4. Dice the apple into tiny cubes and add it to the mixture.
5. Mix it carefully.
6. Preheat the oven to 356 F (180° C), pour the mixture into a mold and bake for approximately 30 minutes, until golden brown.
7. Let it cool down completely, then serve or freeze in portions.

*You can also try this recipe in the raw meat version.

PORK, CHICKEN & PUMPKIN

Ingredients:

- 14 oz pork loin (400 g)
- 10.6 oz chicken breast (300 g)
- 3.5 oz offal (1.1 oz g chicken liver, 0.7 oz chicken heart, 1.7 oz chicken gizzard) (100 g)
- 7 oz pumpkin (200 g)

Nutrition Facts
(Analytical components in 100g):

- Energy   137 kcal
- Fat   4.8 g
- Carbohydrate   1 g
- Fiber   0.2 g
- Protein   19.7 g

Preparation:

1. Prepare ingredients at room temperature. Remove all the skin and fat from the meat. Remove bones, **NEVER** feed pork raw. Rinse meat carefully.
2. Clean liver, heart, and gizzard thoroughly, soak them in cold water, and remove connective tissues.
3. Cut meat and offal into cubes and feed them through a meat grinder.
4. Dice pumpkin into tiny cubes and add it to the mixture.
5. Mix it carefully.
6. Preheat the oven to 356 F (180° C), pour the mixture into a mold and bake for approximately 30 minutes, until golden brown.
7. Let it cool down completely, then serve or freeze in portions.

PUPLOAF

In this section, you will find simple and quick puploaf recipes that are easy to make. They are suitable for all breeds and sizes and should be served cooked, as they contain high-quality grains. Please remember not to add any bones to the food and provide calcium supplementation according to your dog's individual needs.

TO MAKE CORRECT PORTIONS:

Every recipe provided in this section is well-balanced, and you will always find the nutritional analysis at the end. However, the most important factor to consider is the calorie intake because based on that, you can easily calculate the correct daily portion for your dog.

Let's take an example: if your dog has a daily energy requirement (DER) of 630 kcal/day and the recipe you are preparing contains 148 kcal per 100 g, you can use this simple formula to determine the appropriate portion:

Daily Meal Portion (g) = 100 x DER / Meal kcal

e.g., Daily Meal Portion (g) = 100 x 630 / 148 = 425 g (15 oz)

Remember that **knowing your dog's calorie requirement is essential to help them maintain their ideal weight.** You can use the information found in this book, specifically in the chapter titled "Feeding Guidelines & Calorie Calculation," or seek assistance from a veterinarian for added assurance.

CHICKEN, CARROT & RICE

Ingredients:

- 14 oz chicken thighs (400 g)
- 5.3 oz chicken breast (150 g)
- 3.5 oz offal (1.1 oz chicken liver, 0.7 oz chicken heart, 1.7 oz chicken gizzard) (100 g)
- 5.3 oz white rice (150 g)
- 7 oz carrot (200 g)

Nutrition Facts
(Analytical components in 100g):

- Energy   134 kcal
- Fat   5.1 g
- Carbohydrate   6.1 g
- Fiber   0.7 g
- Protein   15.7 g

Preparation:

1. Prepare ingredients at room temperature. Remove half the skin and fat from the thighs and breast. Remove bones if you're going to bake the loaf. Rinse meat carefully.
2. Clean liver, heart, and gizzard thoroughly, soak them in cold water, and remove connective tissues.
3. Cut thighs, breast, offal into cubes and feed them through a meat grinder. Cook in water (slightly covering the meat).
4. Dice carrot into tiny cubes and add it to the mixture.
5. Cook rice according to the label, add to the mixture so rice can soak up the liquid.
6. Mix it carefully.
7. Let it cool down completely, then serve or freeze in portions.

CHICKEN, SWEET POTATO & MILLET

Ingredients:

- 14 oz chicken thighs (400 g)
- 5.3 oz chicken breast (150 g)
- 3.5 oz offal (1.1 oz chicken liver, 0.7 oz chicken heart, 1.7 oz chicken gizzard) (100 g)
- 5.3 oz millet (150 g)
- 7 oz sweet potato (200 g)

Nutrition Facts
(Analytical components in 100g):

- Energy   146 kcal
- Fat   5.2 g
- Carbohydrate   5.1 g
- Fiber   0.9 g
- Protein   15.7 g

Preparation:

1. Prepare ingredients at room temperature. Remove half the skin and fat from the thighs and breast. Remove bones if you're going to bake the loaf. Rinse meat carefully.
2. Clean liver, heart, and gizzard thoroughly, soak them in cold water, and remove connective tissues.
3. Cut thighs, breast, offal into cubes and feed them through a meat grinder. Cook in water (slightly covering the meat).
4. Dice sweet potato into tiny cubes and add it to the mixture.
5. Cook millet according to the label, add to the mixture so millet can soak up the liquid.
6. Mix it carefully.
7. Let it cool down completely, then serve or freeze in portions.

CHICKEN, PUMPKIN & BUCKWHEAT

Ingredients:

- 14 oz chicken thighs (400 g)
- 5.3 oz chicken breast (150 g)
- 3.5 oz offal (1.1 oz chicken liver, 0.7 oz chicken heart, 1.7 oz chicken gizzard) (100 g)
- 5.3 oz buckwheat (150 g)
- 7 oz pumpkin (200 g)

Nutrition Facts
(Analytical components in 100g):

- Energy   135 kcal
- Fat   5.6 g
- Carbohydrate   5.2 g
- Fiber   0.8 g
- Protein   16.5 g

Preparation:

1. Prepare ingredients at room temperature. Remove half the skin and fat from the thighs and breast. Remove bones if you're going to bake the loaf. Rinse meat carefully.
2. Clean liver, heart, and gizzard thoroughly, soak them in cold water, and remove connective tissues.
3. Cut thighs, breast, offal into cubes and feed them through a meat grinder. Cook in water (slightly covering the meat).
4. Dice pumpkin into tiny cubes and add it to the mixture.
5. Cook buckwheat according to the label, add to the mixture so it can soak up the liquid.
6. Mix it carefully.
7. Let it cool down completely, then serve or freeze in portions.

CHICKEN, BEETROOT & BROWN RICE

Ingredients:

- 14 oz chicken thighs (400 g)
- 5.3 oz chicken breast (150 g)
- 3.5 oz offal (1.1 oz chicken liver, 0.7 oz chicken heart, 1.7 oz chicken gizzard) (100 g)
- 5.3 oz brown rice (150 g)
- 7 oz beetroot (200 g)

Nutrition Facts
(Analytical components in 100g):

- Energy   141 kcal
- Fat   5.8 g
- Carbohydrate   4.8 g
- Fiber   0.8 g
- Protein   16.5 g

Preparation:

1. Prepare ingredients at room temperature. Remove all the skin and fat from the thighs and breast. Remove bones if you're going to bake the loaf. Rinse meat carefully.
2. Clean liver, heart, and gizzard thoroughly, soak them in cold water, and remove connective tissues.
3. Cut thighs, breast, offal into cubes and feed them through a meat grinder. Cook in water (slightly covering the meat).
4. Dice beetroot into tiny cubes and add it to the mixture.
5. Cook brown rice according to the label, add to the mixture so it can soak up the liquid.
6. Mix it carefully.
7. Let it cool down completely, then serve or freeze in portions.

CHICKEN, VEGGIE & RICE

Ingredients:

- 14 oz chicken thighs (400 g)
- 5.3 oz chicken breast (150 g)
- 3.5 oz offal (1.1 oz chicken liver, 0.7 oz chicken heart, 1.7 oz chicken gizzard) (100 g)
- 5.3 oz white rice (150 g)
- 3.5 oz carrot (100 g)
- 3.5 oz pumpkin (100 g)

Nutrition Facts
(Analytical components in 100g):

- Energy   142 kcal
- Fat   5.4 g
- Carbohydrate   5.2 g
- Fiber   0.8 g
- Protein   16.8 g

Preparation:

1. Prepare ingredients at room temperature. Remove half the skin and fat from the thighs and breast. Remove bones if you're going to bake the loaf. Rinse meat carefully.
2. Clean liver, heart, and gizzard thoroughly, soak them in cold water, and remove connective tissues.
3. Cut thighs, breast, offal into cubes and feed them through a meat grinder. Cook in water (slightly covering the meat).
4. Dice carrot and pumpkin into tiny cubes and add it to the mixture.
5. Cook rice according to the label, add to the mixture so it can soak up the liquid.
6. Mix it carefully.
7. Let it cool down completely, then serve or freeze in portions.

CHICKEN, VEGGIE & BUCKWHEAT

Ingredients:

- 14 oz chicken thighs (400 g)
- 5.3 oz chicken breast (150 g)
- 3.5 oz offal (1.1 oz chicken liver, 0.7 oz chicken heart, 1.7 oz chicken gizzard) (100 g)
- 5.3 oz buckwheat (150 g)
- 3.5 oz carrot (100 g)
- 3.5 oz sweet potato (100 g)

Nutrition Facts
(Analytical components in 100g):

- Energy   132 kcal
- Fat   5.9 g
- Carbohydrate   5.1 g
- Fiber   0.9 g
- Protein   16.7 g

Preparation:

1. Prepare ingredients at room temperature. Remove all the skin and fat from the thighs and breast. Remove bones if you're going to bake the loaf. Rinse meat carefully.
2. Clean liver, heart, and gizzard thoroughly, soak them in cold water, and remove connective tissues.
3. Cut thighs, breast, offal into cubes and feed them through a meat grinder. Cook in water (slightly covering the meat).
4. Dice carrot and sweet potato into tiny cubes and add it to the mixture.
5. Cook buckwheat according to the label, add to the mixture so it can soak up the liquid.
6. Mix it carefully.
7. Let it cool down completely, then serve or freeze in portions.

CHICKEN, VEGGIE & BROWN RICE

Ingredients:

- 14 oz chicken thighs (400 g)
- 5.3 oz chicken breast (150 g)
- 3.5 oz offal (1.1 oz chicken liver, 0.7 oz chicken heart, 1.7 oz chicken gizzard) (100 g)
- 5.3 oz brown rice (150 g)
- 3.5 oz carrot (100 g)
- 3.5 oz broccoli (100 g)

Nutrition Facts
(Analytical components in 100g):

- Energy   128 kcal
- Fat   4.5 g
- Carbohydrate   3.4 g
- Fiber   0.7 g
- Protein   16.7 g

Preparation:

1. Prepare ingredients at room temperature. Remove all the skin and fat from the thighs and breast. Remove bones if you're going to bake the loaf. Rinse meat carefully.
2. Clean liver, heart, and gizzard thoroughly, soak them in cold water, and remove connective tissues.
3. Cut thighs, breast, offal into cubes and feed them through a meat grinder. Cook in water (slightly covering the meat).
4. Cut broccoli and carrot into tiny cubes and add it to the mixture.
5. Cook brown rice according to the label, add to the mixture so it can soak up the liquid.
6. Mix it carefully.
7. Let it cool down completely, then serve or freeze in portions.

CHICKEN, ROOT VEGGIES & RICE

Ingredients:

- 14 oz chicken thighs (400 g)
- 5.3 oz chicken breast (150 g)
- 3.5 oz offal (1.1 oz chicken liver, 0.7 oz chicken heart, 1.7 oz chicken gizzard) (100 g)
- 5.3 oz white rice (150 g)
- 3.5 oz carrot (100 g)
- 3.5 oz beetroot (100 g)

Nutrition Facts
(Analytical components in 100g):

- Energy   132 kcal
- Fat   4.5 g
- Carbohydrate   3.3 g
- Fiber   0.7 g
- Protein   16.7 g

Preparation:

1. Prepare ingredients at room temperature. Remove all the skin and fat from the thighs and breast. Remove bones if you're going to bake the loaf. Rinse meat carefully.
2. Clean liver, heart, and gizzard thoroughly, soak them in cold water, and remove connective tissues.
3. Cut thighs, breast, offal into cubes and feed them through a meat grinder. Cook in water (slightly covering the meat).
4. Cut beetroot and carrot into tiny cubes and add it to the mixture.
5. Cook rice according to the label, add to the mixture so it can soak up the liquid.
6. Mix it carefully.
7. Let it cool down completely, then serve or freeze in portions.

CHICKEN, BERRY & MILLET

Ingredients:

- 14 oz chicken thighs (400 g)
- 5.3 oz chicken breast (150 g)
- 3.5 oz offal (1.1 oz chicken liver, 0.7 oz chicken heart, 1.7 oz chicken gizzard) (100 g)
- 5.3 oz millet (150 g)
- 3.5 oz carrot (150 g)
- 1.7 oz blueberries (100 g)

Nutrition Facts
(Analytical components in 100g):

- Energy   137 kcal
- Fat   4.9 g
- Carbohydrate   5.1 g
- Fiber   1.2 g
- Protein   14.7 g

Preparation:

1. Prepare ingredients at room temperature. Remove half the skin and fat from the thighs and breast. Remove bones if you're going to bake the loaf. Rinse meat carefully.
2. Clean liver, heart, and gizzard thoroughly, soak them in cold water, and remove connective tissues.
3. Cut thighs, breast, offal into cubes and feed them through a meat grinder. Cook in water (slightly covering the meat).
4. Cut carrot and blueberries into tiny cubes and add it to the mixture.
5. Cook millet according to the label, add to the mixture so it can soak up the liquid.
6. Mix it carefully.
7. Let it cool down completely, then serve or freeze in portions.

LEAN CHICKEN & RICE

Ingredients:

- 19.4 oz chicken breast (550 g)
- 3.5 oz offal (1.1 oz chicken liver, 0.7 oz chicken heart, 1.7 oz chicken gizzard) (100 g)
- 5.3 oz white rice (150 g)
- 7 oz carrot (200 g)

Nutrition Facts
(Analytical components in 100g):

- Energy   132 kcal
- Fat   2.3 g
- Carbohydrate   3.2 g
- Fiber   0.8 g
- Protein   21.7 g

Preparation:

1. Prepare ingredients at room temperature. Remove all the skin and fat from the breast. Remove bones if you're going to bake the loaf. Rinse meat carefully.
2. Clean liver, heart, and gizzard thoroughly, soak them in cold water, and remove connective tissues.
3. Cut breast and offal into cubes and feed them through a meat grinder. Cook in water (slightly covering the meat).
4. Cut carrot into tiny cubes and add it to the mixture.
5. Cook rice according to the label, add to the mixture so it can soak up the liquid.
6. Mix it carefully.
7. Let it cool down completely, then serve or freeze in portions.

DUCK, CARROT & BUCKWHEAT

Ingredients:

- 19.4 oz duck (550 g)
- 3.5 oz offal (1.1 oz chicken liver, 0.7 oz chicken heart, 1.7 oz chicken gizzard) (100 g)
- 5.3 oz buckwheat (150 g)
- 7 oz carrot (200 g)

Nutrition Facts
(Analytical components in 100g):

- Energy   241 kcal
- Fat   12.6 g
- Carbohydrate   4.2 g
- Fiber   0.9 g
- Protein   13.3 g

Preparation:

1. Prepare ingredients at room temperature. Remove half the skin and fat from the meat. Remove bones if you're going to bake the loaf. Rinse meat carefully.
2. Clean liver, heart, and gizzard thoroughly, soak them in cold water, and remove connective tissues.
3. Cut meat into cubes and feed them through a meat grinder. Cook in water (slightly covering the meat).
4. Cut the carrots into tiny cubes and add it to the mixture.
5. Cook buckwheat according to the label, add to the mixture so it can soak up the liquid.
6. Mix it carefully.
7. Let it cool down completely, then serve or freeze in portions.

POULTRY & RICE

Ingredients:

- 14 oz duck (400 g)
- 5.3 oz chicken breast (150 g)
- 3.5 oz offal (1.1 oz chicken liver, 0.7 oz chicken heart, 1.7 oz chicken gizzard) (100 g)
- 5.3 oz white rice (150 g)
- 7 oz carrot (200 g)

Nutrition Facts
(Analytical components in 100g):

- Energy   251 kcal
- Fat   6.5 g
- Carbohydrate   6.2 g
- Fiber   0.5 g
- Protein   14.5 g

Preparation:

1. Prepare ingredients at room temperature. Remove all the skin and fat from the duck and chicken breast. Remove bones if you're going to bake the loaf. Rinse meat carefully.
2. Clean liver, heart, and gizzard thoroughly, soak them in cold water, and remove connective tissues.
3. Cut duck, chicken breast, offal into cubes and feed them through a meat grinder. Cook in water (slightly covering the meat).
4. Cut carrot into tiny cubes and add it to the mixture.
5. Cook rice according to the label, add to the mixture so it can soak up the liquid.
6. Mix it carefully.
7. Let it cool down completely, then serve or freeze in portions.

DUCK, PUMPKIN, SWEET POTATO & RICE

Ingredients:

- 19.4 oz duck (550 g)
- 3.5 oz offal (1.1 oz chicken liver, 0.7 oz chicken heart, 1.7 oz chicken gizzard) (100 g)
- 5.3 oz rice (150 g)
- 3.5 oz pumpkin (100 g)
- 3.5 oz sweet potato (100 g)

Nutrition Facts
(Analytical components in 100g):

- Energy   315 kcal
- Fat   11 g
- Carbohydrate   6.4 g
- Fiber   0.5 g
- Protein   15.4 g

Preparation:

1. Prepare ingredients at room temperature. Remove all the skin and fat from the duck. Remove bones if you're going to bake the loaf. Rinse meat carefully.
2. Clean liver, heart, and gizzard thoroughly, soak them in cold water, and remove connective tissues.
3. Cut duck and offal into cubes and feed them through a meat grinder. Cook in water (slightly covering the meat).
4. Cut pumpkin and sweet potato into tiny cubes and add it to the mixture.
5. Cook rice according to the label, add to the mixture so it can soak up the liquid.
6. Mix it carefully.
7. Let it cool down completely, then serve or freeze in portions.

BEEF, CARROT & BROWN RICE

Ingredients:

- 12.3 oz beef (350 g)
- 3.5 oz offal (1.7 oz beef liver, 1.8 oz beef heart) (100 g)
- 5.3 oz beef green tripe (150 g)
- 8.8 oz brown rice (250 g)
- 5.3 oz carrot (150 g)

Nutrition Facts
(Analytical components in 100g):

- Energy   185 kcal
- Fat   5.8 g
- Carbohydrate   8.3 g
- Fiber   0.7 g
- Protein   19.3 g

Preparation:

1. Prepare ingredients at room temperature. Remove half the fat from the meat. Remove bones if you're going to bake the loaf. Rinse meat carefully.
2. Clean liver and heart thoroughly, soak them in cold water, and remove connective tissues.
3. Cut meat, green tripe, and offal into cubes and feed them through a meat grinder. Cook in water (slightly covering the meat).
4. Cut carrot into tiny cubes and add it to the mixture.
5. Cook rice according to the label, add to the mixture so it can soak up the liquid.
6. Mix it carefully.
7. Let it cool down completely, then serve or freeze in portions.

BEEF, SWEET POTATO & RICE

Ingredients:

- 12.3 oz beef (lean) (350 g)
- 3.5 oz offal (1.7 oz beef liver, 1.8 oz beef heart) (100 g)
- 5.3 oz beef green tripe (150 g)
- 8.8 oz white rice (250 g)
- 5.3 oz sweet potato (150 g)

Nutrition Facts
(Analytical components in 100g):

- Energy   161 kcal
- Fat   7.3 g
- Carbohydrate   9.1 g
- Fiber   0.8 g
- Protein   19.1 g

Preparation:

1. Prepare ingredients at room temperature. Remove half the fat from the meat. Remove bones if you're going to bake the loaf. Rinse meat carefully.
2. Clean liver and heart thoroughly, soak them in cold water, and remove connective tissues.
3. Cut meat, green tripe, and offal into cubes and feed them through a meat grinder. Cook in water (slightly covering the meat).
4. Cut sweet potato into tiny cubes and add it to the mixture.
5. Cook rice according to the label, add to the mixture so it can soak up the liquid.
6. Mix it carefully.
7. Let it cool down completely, then serve or freeze in portions.

BEEF, PUMPKIN & RICE

Ingredients:

- 12.3 oz beef (350 g)
- 3.5 oz offal (1.7 oz beef liver, 1.8 oz beef heart) (100 g)
- 5.3 oz beef green tripe (150 g)
- 8.8 oz white rice (250 g)
- 5.3 oz pumpkin (150 g)

Nutrition Facts
(Analytical components in 100g):

- Energy   186 kcal
- Fat   7.4 g
- Carbohydrate   5.7 g
- Fiber   0.7 g
- Protein   19.5 g

Preparation:

1. Prepare ingredients at room temperature. Remove half the fat from the meat. Remove bones if you're going to bake the loaf. Rinse meat carefully.
2. Clean liver and heart thoroughly, soak them in cold water, and remove connective tissues.
3. Cut meat, green tripe, and offal into cubes and feed them through a meat grinder. Cook in water (slightly covering the meat).
4. Cut pumpkin into tiny cubes and add it to the mixture.
5. Cook rice according to the label, add to the mixture so it can soak up the liquid.
6. Mix it carefully.
7. Let it cool down completely, then serve or freeze in portions.

BEEF, BEETROOT & BUCKWHEAT

Ingredients:

- 15.9 oz beef (450 g)
- 3.5 oz offal (1.7 oz beef liver, 1.8 oz beef heart) (100 g)
- 5.3 oz beef green tripe (150 g)
- 5.3 oz buckwheat (150 g)
- 5.3 oz beetroot (150 g)

Nutrition Facts
(Analytical components in 100g):

- Energy   176 kcal
- Fat   7.9 g
- Carbohydrate   5.3 g
- Fiber   0.4 g
- Protein   20.1 g

Preparation:

1. Prepare ingredients at room temperature. Remove half the fat from the meat. Remove bones if you're going to bake the loaf. Rinse meat carefully.
2. Clean liver and heart thoroughly, soak them in cold water, and remove connective tissues.
3. Cut meat, green tripe, and offal into cubes and feed them through a meat grinder. Cook in water (slightly covering the meat).
4. Cut beetroot into tiny cubes and add it to the mixture.
5. Cook buckwheat according to the label, add to the mixture so it can soak up the liquid.
6. Mix it carefully.
7. Let it cool down completely, then serve or freeze in portions.

BEEF, VEGGIES & RICE

Ingredients:

- 15.9 oz beef (450 g)
- 3.5 oz offal (1.7 oz beef liver, 1.8 oz beef heart) (100 g)
- 5.3 oz beef green tripe (150 g)
- 5.3 oz white rice (150 g)
- 3.5 oz carrot (100 g)
- 1.7 oz sweet potato (50 g)

Nutrition Facts
(Analytical components in 100g):

- Energy   178 kcal
- Fat   7.8 g
- Carbohydrate   5.6 g
- Fiber   0.4 g
- Protein   20.1 g

Preparation:

1. Prepare ingredients at room temperature. Remove half the fat from the meat. Remove bones if you're going to bake the loaf. Rinse meat carefully.
2. Clean liver and heart thoroughly, soak them in cold water, and remove connective tissues.
3. Cut meat, green tripe, and offal into cubes and feed them through a meat grinder. Cook in water (slightly covering the meat).
4. Cut carrot and sweet potato into tiny cubes and add it to the mixture.
5. Cook white rice according to the label, add to the mixture so it can soak up the liquid.
6. Mix it carefully.
7. Let it cool down completely, then serve or freeze in portions.

BEEF, BEETROOT, SWEET POTATO & RICE

Ingredients:

- 15.9 oz beef (450 g)
- 3.5 oz offal (1.7 oz beef liver, 1.8 oz beef heart) (100 g)
- 5.3 oz beef green tripe (150 g)
- 5.3 oz white rice (150 g)
- 3.5 oz sweet potato (100 g)
- 1.7 oz beetroot (50 g)

Nutrition Facts
(Analytical components in 100g):

- Energy   177 kcal
- Fat   7.6 g
- Carbohydrate   5.6 g
- Fiber   0.7 g
- Protein   20.1 g

Preparation:

1. Prepare ingredients at room temperature. Remove half the fat from the meat. Remove bones if you're going to bake the loaf. Rinse meat carefully.
2. Clean liver and heart thoroughly, soak them in cold water, and remove connective tissues.
3. Cut meat, green tripe, and offal into cubes and feed them through a meat grinder. Cook in water (slightly covering the meat).
4. Cut beetroot and sweet potato into tiny cubes and add it to the mixture.
5. Cook white rice according to the label, add to the mixture so it can soak up the liquid.
6. Mix it carefully.
7. Let it cool down completely, then serve or freeze in portions.

LEAN BEEF, CARROT & RICE

Ingredients:

- 19.4 oz beef (lean) (550 g)
- 3.5 oz offal (1.7 oz beef liver, 1.8 oz beef heart) (100 g)
- 5.3 oz white rice (150 g)
- 7 oz carrot (200 g)

Nutrition Facts
(Analytical components in 100g):

- Energy   156 kcal
- Fat   6.2 g
- Carbohydrate   5.8 g
- Fiber   0.8 g
- Protein   20.3 g

Preparation:

1. Prepare ingredients at room temperature. Remove half the fat from the meat. Remove bones if you're going to bake the loaf. Rinse meat carefully.
2. Clean liver and heart thoroughly, soak them in cold water, and remove connective tissues.
3. Cut meat and offal into cubes and feed them through a meat grinder. Cook in water (slightly covering the meat).
4. Cut carrot into tiny cubes and add it to the mixture.
5. Cook white rice according to the label, add to the mixture so it can soak up the liquid.
6. Mix it carefully.
7. Let it cool down completely, then serve or freeze in portions.

LEAN BEEF, SWEET POTATO & MILLET

Ingredients:

- 19.4 oz beef (lean) (550 g)
- 3.5 oz offal (1.7 oz beef liver, 1.8 oz beef heart) (100 g)
- 5.3 oz millet (150 g)
- 7 oz sweet potato (200 g)

Preparation:

1. Prepare ingredients at room temperature. Remove half the fat from the meat. Remove bones if you're going to bake the loaf. Rinse meat carefully.
2. Clean liver and heart thoroughly, soak them in cold water, and remove connective tissues.
3. Cut meat and offal into cubes and feed them through a meat grinder. Cook in water (slightly covering the meat).
4. Cut sweet potato into tiny cubes and add it to the mixture.
5. Cook white rice according to the label, add to the mixture so it can soak up the liquid.
6. Mix it carefully.
7. Let it cool down completely, then serve or freeze in portions.

Nutrition Facts
(Analytical components in 100g):

- Energy   157 kcal
- Fat   6.3 g
- Carbohydrate 5.5 g
- Fiber   0.7 g
- Protein   20.2 g

RABBIT, CARROT & BROWN RICE

Ingredients:

- 14 oz rabbit (400 g)
- 3.5 oz offal (1.7 oz rabbit liver, 1.8 oz rabbit heart) (100 g)
- 12.3 oz brown rice (350 g)
- 5.3 oz carrot (150 g)

Preparation:

1. Prepare ingredients at room temperature. Rinse meat carefully.
2. Clean liver and heart thoroughly, then soak them in cold water and remove connective tissues.
3. Cut meat, offal into cubes and feed them through a meat grinder. Cook in water (slightly covering the meat).
4. Cook brown rice according to the package label, add to the mixture to soak up the liquid..
5. Dice carrot into tiny cubes, steam it, and add it to the mixture.
6. Mix it carefully.
7. Freeze in portions.

Nutrition Facts
(Analytical components in 100g):

- Energy   146 kcal
- Fat   3.6 g
- Carbohydrate 9.6 g
- Fiber   1.1 g
- Protein   15.2 g

RABBIT, PUMPKIN & BUCKWHEAT

Ingredients:

- 15.9 oz rabbit (450 g)
- 3.5 offal (1.1 oz chicken liver, 0.7 oz chicken heart, 1.7 oz chicken gizzard) (100 g)
- 8.8 oz buckwheat (250 g)
- 7 oz pumpkin (200 g)

Nutrition Facts
(Analytical components in 100g):

- Energy   156 kcal
- Fat   5.9 g
- Carbohydrate   5.1 g
- Fiber   0.4 g
- Protein   22.3 g

Preparation:

1. Prepare ingredients at room temperature. Remove any fat from the meat. Remove bones. Rinse meat carefully.
2. Clean liver, heart, and gizzard thoroughly, soak them in cold water, and remove connective tissues.
3. Cut meat and offal into cubes and feed them through a meat grinder. Cook in water (slightly covering the meat).
4. Cook buckwheat according to the package label, add to the mixture to soak up the liquid.
5. Dice pumpkin into tiny cubes and add it to the mixture.
6. Mix it carefully.
7. Let it cool down completely, then serve or freeze in portions.

RABBIT, CHICKEN & MILLET

Ingredients:

- 7 oz rabbit (200 g)
- 10.6 oz chicken breast (300 g)
- 3.5 offal (1.1 oz chicken liver, 0.7 oz chicken heart, 1.7 oz chicken gizzard) (100 g)
- 7 oz millet (200 g)
- 7 oz carrot (200 g)

Nutrition Facts
(Analytical components in 100g):

- Energy   152 kcal
- Fat   3.8 g
- Carbohydrate   5.2 g
- Fiber   0.7 g
- Protein   18.6 g

Preparation:

1. Prepare ingredients at room temperature. Remove all the skin and fat from the meat. Remove bones. Rinse meat carefully.
2. Clean liver, heart, and gizzard thoroughly, soak them in cold water, and remove connective tissues.
3. Cut meat and offal into cubes and feed them through a meat grinder. Cook in water (slightly covering the meat)
4. Cook millet according to the package label, add to the mixture to soak up the liquid.
5. Dice carrot into tiny cubes and add it to the mixture.
6. Mix it carefully.
7. Let it cool down completely, then serve or freeze in portions.

RABBIT, APPLE & BROWN RICE

Ingredients:

- 14 oz rabbit (400 g)
- 3.5 offal (1.1 oz chicken liver, 0.7 oz chicken heart, 1.7 oz chicken gizzard) (100 g)
- 10.6 oz brown rice (300 g)
- 7 oz apple (200 g)

Nutrition Facts
(Analytical components in 100g):

- Energy   161 kcal
- Fat   4.4 g
- Carbohydrate   8.8 g
- Fiber   0.9 g
- Protein   16.4 g

Preparation:

1. Prepare ingredients at room temperature. Remove any fat from the meat. Remove bones. Rinse meat carefully.
2. Clean liver, heart, and gizzard thoroughly, soak them in cold water, and remove connective tissues.
3. Cut meat and offal into cubes and feed them through a meat grinder. Cook in water (slightly covering the meat).
4. Cook brown rice according to the package label, add to the mixture to soak up the liquid.
5. Dice apple into tiny cubes and add it to the mixture.
6. Mix it carefully.
7. Let it cool down completely, then serve or freeze in portions.

LAMB & GRAINS

Ingredients:

- 10.6 oz lamb (300 g)
- 3.5 oz offal (1.7 oz lamb liver, 1.8 oz lamb heart) (100 g)
- 1.7 oz green tripe (lamb) (optional) (50 g)
- 8.8 oz brown rice (250 g)
- 5.3 oz quinoa (150 g)
- 3.5 oz pumpkin (100 g)
- 1.7 oz carrot (50 g)

Nutrition Facts
(Analytical components in 100g):

- Energy   162 kcal
- Fat   8.1 g
- Carbohydrate   10.3 g
- Fiber   1.1 g
- Protein   12 g

Preparation:

1. Prepare ingredients at room temperature. Rinse meat carefully.
2. Clean liver and heart thoroughly, soak them in cold water, and remove connective tissues.
3. Cut meat, green tripe, and offal into cubes and feed them through a meat grinder. Cook in water (slightly covering the meat).
4. Cook brown rice and quinoa according to the packaging label.
5. Peel, then dice pumpkin and carrot into tiny cubes and steam/bake (dried pumpkin and carrot is also a great option, but make sure it's additive free and not salted).
6. Add cooked pumpkin and carrot to the mixture, incorporating it carefully.
7. Freeze in portions.

LEAN LAMB, CARROT & RICE

Ingredients:
- 19.4 oz lamb (lean) (550 g)
- 3.5 oz offal (1.7 oz lamb liver, 1.8 oz lamb heart) (100 g)
- 5.3 oz white rice (150 g)
- 7 oz carrot (200 g)

Preparation:
1. Prepare ingredients at room temperature. Rinse meat carefully.
2. Clean liver and heart thoroughly, soak them in cold water, and remove connective tissues.
3. Cut meat and offal into cubes and feed them through a meat grinder. Cook in water (slightly covering the meat).
4. Cook white rice according to the packaging label.
5. Peel, then dice carrot into tiny cubes and steam/bake (dried carrot is also a great option, but make sure it's additive-free and not salted).
6. Add steamed carrot to the mixture, incorporating it carefully.
7. Freeze in portions.

Nutrition Facts
(Analytical components in 100g):

- Energy   132 kcal
- Fat   5.6 g
- Carbohydrate   4.9 g
- Fiber   0.8 g
- Protein   19.2 g

LEAN LAMB, SWEET POTATO & RICE

Ingredients:
- 19.4 oz lamb (lean) (550 g)
- 3.5 oz offal (1.7 oz lamb liver, 1.8 oz lamb heart) (100 g)
- 5.3 oz white rice (150 g)
- 7 oz sweet potato (200 g)

Preparation:
1. Prepare ingredients at room temperature. Rinse meat carefully.
2. Clean liver and heart thoroughly, soak them in cold water, and remove connective tissues.
3. Cut meat and offal into cubes and feed them through a meat grinder. Cook in water (slightly covering the meat).
4. Cook white rice according to the packaging label.
5. Peel, then dice sweet potatoes into tiny cubes and steam/bake.
6. Add cooked sweet potato to the mixture, incorporating it carefully.
7. Freeze in portions.

Nutrition Facts
(Analytical components in 100g):

- Energy   134 kcal
- Fat   5.7 g
- Carbohydrate   4.5 g
- Fiber   0.6 g
- Protein   21.4 g

LAMB, SALMON & RICE

Ingredients:

- 19.4 oz lamb (550 g)
- 3.5 oz offal (1.7 oz lamb liver, 1.8 oz lamb heart) (100 g)
- 3.5 oz white rice (100 g)
- 5.3 oz salmon (boneless) (150 g)
- 3.5 oz carrot (100 g)

Nutrition Facts
(Analytical components in 100g):

- Energy   224 kcal
- Fat   14.9 g
- Carbohydrate   10.4 g
- Fiber   1.4 g
- Protein   20.4 g

Preparation:

1. Prepare ingredients at room temperature. Rinse meat carefully.
2. Clean liver and heart thoroughly, soak them in cold water, and remove connective tissues.
3. Cut lamb, salmon, and offal into cubes and feed them through a meat grinder (optionally you can feed meat in bigger chunks, too). Cook in water (slightly covering the meat).
4. Cook white rice according to the packaging label.
5. Dice carrot into tiny cubes, and add it to the mixture.
6. Mix it carefully.
7. Freeze in portions.

LAMB, SALMON & BROWN RICE

Ingredients:

- 19.4 oz lamb (550 g)
- 3.5 oz offal (1.7 oz lamb liver, 1.8 oz lamb heart) (100 g)
- 3.5 oz brown rice (100 g)
- 5.3 oz salmon (boneless) (150 g)
- 3.5 oz carrot (100 g)

Nutrition Facts
(Analytical components in 100g):

- Energy   220 kcal
- Fat   14.8 g
- Carbohydrate   9.8 g
- Fiber   1.8 g
- Protein   20.6 g

Preparation:

1. Prepare ingredients at room temperature. Rinse meat carefully.
2. Clean liver and heart thoroughly, soak them in cold water, and remove connective tissues.
3. Cut lamb, salmon, and offal into cubes and feed them through a meat grinder (optionally you can feed meat in bigger chunks, too). Cook in water (slightly covering the meat).
4. Cook brown rice according to the packaging label.
5. Dice carrot into tiny cubes, and add it to the mixture.
6. Mix it carefully.
7. Freeze in portions.

LAMB, SALMON & MILLET

Ingredients:

- 19.4 oz lamb (550 g)
- 3.5 oz offal (1.7 oz lamb liver, 1.8 oz lamb heart) (100 g)
- 3.5 oz millet (100 g)
- 5.3 oz salmon (boneless) (150 g)
- 3.5 oz carrot (100 g)

Preparation:

1. Prepare ingredients at room temperature. Rinse meat carefully.
2. Clean liver and heart thoroughly, soak them in cold water, and remove connective tissues.
3. Cut lamb, salmon, and offal into cubes and feed them through a meat grinder (optionally you can feed meat in bigger chunks, too). Cook in water (slightly covering the meat).
4. Cook millet according to the packaging label.
5. Dice carrot into tiny cubes, and add it to the mixture.
6. Mix it carefully.
7. Freeze in portions.

Nutrition Facts
(Analytical components in 100g):

- Energy   221 kcal
- Fat 1   4.6 g
- Carbohydrate 9.4 g
- Fiber   1.7 g
- Protein   20.3 g

LAMB, SALMON & BUCKWHEAT

Ingredients:

- 19.4 oz lamb (550 g)
- 3.5 oz offal (1.7 oz lamb liver, 1.8 oz lamb heart) (100 g)
- 3.5 oz buckwheat (100 g)
- 5.3 oz salmon (boneless) (150 g)
- 3.5 oz carrot (100 g)

Preparation:

1. Prepare ingredients at room temperature. Rinse meat carefully.
2. Clean liver and heart thoroughly, soak them in cold water, and remove connective tissues.
3. Cut lamb, salmon, and offal into cubes and feed them through a meat grinder (optionally you can feed meat in bigger chunks, too). Cook in water (slightly covering the meat).
4. Cook brown rice according to the packaging label.
5. Dice carrot into tiny cubes, and add it to the mixture.
6. Mix it carefully.
7. Freeze in portions.

Nutrition Facts
(Analytical components in 100g):

- Energy   219 kcal
- Fat   14.8 g
- Carbohydrate 9.7 g
- Fiber   1.9 g
- Protein   20.2 g

GOAT, VENISON & WHITE RICE

Ingredients:

- 14 oz goat (400 g)
- 10.6 oz venison (300 g)
- 3.5 oz offal (1.7 oz venison liver, 1.7 oz venison heart) (100 g)
- 3.5 oz white rice (100 g)
- 3.5 oz beetroot (100 g)

Preparation:

1. Prepare ingredients at room temperature. Rinse meat carefully.
2. Clean liver and heart thoroughly, soak them in cold water, and remove connective tissues.
3. Cut meat and offal into cubes and feed them through a meat grinder (optionally you can feed meat in bigger chunks, too). Cook in water (slightly covering the meat).
4. Cook white rice according to the packaging label.
5. Dice beetroot into tiny cubes, and add it to the mixture.
6. Mix it carefully.
7. Freeze in portions.

Nutrition Facts
(Analytical components in 100g):

- Energy   131 kcal
- Fat   2.7 g
- Carbohydrate 6.7 g
- Fiber   0.6 g
- Protein   23.2 g

LAMB, VENISON & QUINOA

Ingredients:

- 14 oz lamb (400 g)
- 10.6 oz venison (300 g)
- 3.5 oz offal (1.7 oz venison liver, 1.7 oz venison heart) (100 g)
- 3.5 oz quinoa (100 g)
- 3.5 oz beetroot (100 g)

Preparation:

1. Prepare ingredients at room temperature. Rinse meat carefully.
2. Clean liver and heart thoroughly, soak them in cold water, and remove connective tissues.
3. Cut meat and offal into cubes and feed them through a meat grinder (optionally you can feed meat in bigger chunks, too). Cook in water (slightly covering the meat).
4. Cook quinoa according to the packaging label.
5. Dice beetroot into tiny cubes, and add it to the mixture.
6. Mix it carefully.
7. Freeze in portions.

Nutrition Facts
(Analytical components in 100g):

- Energy   128 kcal
- Fat   2.6 g
- Carbohydrate 6.3 g
- Fiber   0.8 g
- Protein   23.1 g

DUCK, SALMON & MILLET

Ingredients:

- 12.3 oz duck (350 g)
- 3.5 g offal (1,7 oz duck liver, 1,8 oz duck heart) (100 g)
- 10.6 oz salmon (boneless) (300 g)
- 3.5 g millet (100 g)
- 3.5 g carrot (100 g)
- 1.7 oz broccoli (50 g)

Nutrition Facts
(Analytical components in 100g):

- Energy   214 kcal
- Fat   12.9 g
- Carbohydrate   5.3 g
- Fiber   0.2 g
- Protein   14.6 g

Preparation:

1. Prepare ingredients at room temperature. Rinse meat carefully.
2. Clean liver and heart thoroughly, soak them in cold water, and remove connective tissues.
3. Cut meat and offal into cubes and feed them through a meat grinder (optionally you can feed meat in bigger chunks, too). Cook in water (slightly covering the meat).
4. Cook millet according to the packaging label.
5. Dice carrot and broccoli into tiny cubes, and add it to the mixture.
6. Mix it carefully.
7. Freeze in portions.

CHICKEN & GRAINS

Ingredients:

- 12.3 oz chicken thighs (350 g)
- 3.5 oz offal (1.7 oz chicken liver, 1.8 oz chicken heart) (100 g)
- 8.8 oz white rice (250 g)
- 5.3 oz millet (150 g)
- 3.5 oz carrot (100 g)
- 1.7 oz apple (optional) (50 g)

Nutrition Facts
(Analytical components in 100g):

- Energy   125 kcal
- Fat   3.7 g
- Carbohydrate   10.3 g
- Fiber   1.1 g
- Protein   7.1 g

Preparation:

1. Prepare ingredients at room temperature. Rinse meat carefully, remove bones.
2. Clean offal thoroughly, soak in cold water, and remove connective tissues.
3. Cut meat and offal into cubes and feed them through a meat grinder. Cook in water (slightly covering the meat)
4. Cook rice and millet according to the packaging label.
5. Peel, then dice carrot and apple into tiny cubes and steam/bake (dried carrot is also a great option, but make sure it's additive free and not salted).
6. Add cooked carrot and apple to the mixture, incorporating it carefully.
7. Freeze in portions.

VENISON & GRAINS

Ingredients:

- 12.3 oz venison (350 g)
- 3.5 oz offal (1.7 oz venison liver, 1.8 oz venison heart) (100 g)
- 8.8 oz white rice (250 g)
- 5.3 oz millet (150 g)
- 3.5 oz carrot (100 g)
- 1.7 oz blueberries (optional) (50 g)

Nutrition Facts
(Analytical components in 100g):

- Energy   162 kcal
- Fat   8.1 g
- Carbohydrate   10.3 g
- Fiber   1.1 g
- Protein   12 g

Preparation:

1. Prepare ingredients at room temperature. Rinse meat carefully.
2. Clean offal thoroughly, soak in cold water, and remove connective tissues.
3. Cut meat and offal into cubes and feed them through a meat grinder. Cook in water (slightly covering the meat)
4. Cook rice and millet according to the packaging label.
5. Peel, then dice carrot into tiny cubes and steam/bake (dried carrot is also a great option, but make sure it's additive free and not salted).
6. Add cooked carrot and blueberries to the mixture, incorporating it carefully.
7. Freeze in portions.

CHICKEN, BEEF & BUCKWHEAT

Ingredients:

- 10.6 oz chicken breast (300 g)
- 10.6 oz beef (300 g)
- 3.5 oz offal (1.7 oz beef liver, 1.7 oz beef heart) (100 g)
- 5.3 oz buckwheat (150 g)
- 3.5 oz pumpkin (100 g)
- 1.7 oz beetroot (50 g)

Nutrition Facts
(Analytical components in 100g):

- Energy   131 kcal
- Fat   4.7 g
- Carbohydrate   3.7 g
- Fiber   0.5 g
- Protein   17.7 g

Preparation:

1. Prepare ingredients at room temperature. Rinse meat carefully.
2. Clean offal thoroughly, soak in cold water, and remove connective tissues.
3. Cut meat and offal into cubes and feed them through a meat grinder. Cook in water (slightly covering the meat)
4. Cook buckwheat according to the packaging label.
5. Peel and dice pumpkin and beetroot into tiny cubes and steam/bake.
6. Add cooked pumpkin and beetroot to the mixture, incorporating it carefully.
7. Let it cool down completely, then serve or freeze in portions.

MEAT MIX & WHITE RICE

Ingredients:

- 10.6 oz chicken breast (300 g)
- 10.6 oz lamb (300 g)
- 3.5 oz offal (1.7 oz beef liver, 1.8 oz beef heart) (100 g)
- 5.3 oz white rice (150 g)
- 3.5 oz carrot (100 g)
- 1.7 beetroot (50 g)

Nutrition Facts
(Analytical components in 100g):

- Energy   170 kcal
- Fat   8.7 g
- Carbohydrate 5.3 g
- Fiber   0.6 g
- Protein   18.7 g

Preparation:

1. Prepare ingredients at room temperature. Rinse meat carefully.
2. Clean offal thoroughly, soak in cold water, and remove connective tissues.
3. Cut meat and offal into cubes and feed them through a meat grinder. Cook in water (slightly covering the meat).
4. Cook white rice according to the packaging label, add to mixture to soak up the liquid.
5. Peel, then dice carrot and beetroot and into tiny cubes and steam/bake.
6. Add cooked carrot and beetroot to the mixture, incorporating it carefully.
7. Let it cool down completely, then serve or freeze in portions.

TURKEY, APPLE & WHITE RICE

Ingredients:

- 14 oz turkey breast (400 g)
- 3.5 oz offal (1.1 oz chicken liver, 0.7 oz chicken heart, 1.7 oz chicken gizzard) (100 g)
- 10.6 oz white rice (300 g)
- 3.5 oz carrot (100 g)
- 3.5 oz apple (100 g)

Nutrition Facts
(Analytical components in 100g):

- Energy   129 kcal
- Fat   1.4 g
- Carbohydrate 9.5 g
- Fiber   0.9 g
- Protein   15.6 g

Preparation:

1. Prepare ingredients at room temperature. Remove all the skin and fat from the meat. Remove bones if you're going to bake the loaf. Rinse meat carefully.
2. Clean liver, heart, and gizzard thoroughly, soak them in cold water, and remove connective tissues.
3. Cut meat and offal into cubes and feed them through a meat grinder. Cook in water (slightly covering the meat).
4. Cook rice according to the packaging label, add to mixture to soak up the liquid.
5. Dice carrot and apple into tiny cubes and add it to the mixture.
6. Mix it carefully.
7. Let it cool down completely, then serve or freeze in portions.

SALMON, CARROT & BROWN RICE

Ingredients:

- 17.6 oz salmon (500 g)
- 3.5 oz offal (1.1 oz chicken liver, 0.7 oz chicken heart, 1.7 oz chicken gizzard) (100 g)
- 200 g brown rice (200 g)
- 200 g carrot (200 g)

Nutrition Facts
(Analytical components in 100g):

- Energy   171 kcal
- Fat   7.8 g
- Carbohydrate   8.2 g
- Fiber   1.1 g
- Protein   16.7 g

Preparation:

1. Prepare ingredients at room temperature. Remove bones. Rinse salmon carefully.
2. Clean liver, heart, and gizzard thoroughly, soak them in cold water, and remove connective tissues.
3. Cut salmon and offal into cubes and feed them through a meat grinder. Cook in water (slightly covering the meat).
4. Cook brown rice according to the packaging label, add to mixture to soak up the liquid.
5. Dice carrot into tiny cubes and add it to the mixture.
6. Mix it carefully.
7. Let it cool down completely, then serve or freeze in portions.

PORK, CHICKEN & BUCKWHEAT

Ingredients:

- 14 oz pork (400 g)
- 7 oz chicken breast (200 g)
- 3.5 oz offal (1.1 oz chicken liver, 0.7 oz chicken heart, 1.7 oz chicken gizzard) (100 g)
- 3.5 oz buckwheat (100 g)
- 3.5 oz pumpkin (100 g)
- 2 eggs

Nutrition Facts
(Analytical components in 100g):

- Energy   137 kcal
- Fat   4.7 g
- Carbohydrate   3.1 g
- Fiber   0.5 g
- Protein   17.7 g

Preparation:

1. Prepare ingredients at room temperature. Remove half the skin and fat from the meat. Remove bones. Rinse meat carefully.
2. Clean liver, heart, and gizzard thoroughly, soak them in cold water, and remove connective tissues.
3. Cut meat and offal into cubes and feed them through a meat grinder. Cook in water (slightly covering the meat).
4. Cook buckwheat according to the label, add to mixture to soak up liquid. Add eggs.
5. Dice pumpkin into tiny cubes and add it to the mixture.
6. Mix it carefully.
7. Let it cool down completely, then serve or freeze in portions.

CHICKEN, KANGAROO & WHITE RICE

Ingredients:

- 7 oz chicken breast (200 g)
- 12.3 oz kangaroo (350 g)
- 3.5 oz offal (1.1 oz chicken liver, 0.7 oz chicken heart, 1.7 oz chicken gizzard) (100 g)
- 7 oz white rice (200 g)
- 3.5 oz carrot (100 g)
- 1.7 oz blueberries (50 g)

Nutrition Facts
(Analytical components in 100g):

- Energy   137 kcal
- Fat   3.3 g
- Carbohydrate 8.9 g
- Fiber   0.8 g
- Protein   21.6 g

Preparation:

1. Prepare ingredients at room temperature. Remove half the skin and fat from the breast. Remove bones. Rinse meat carefully.
2. Clean liver, heart, and gizzard thoroughly, soak them in cold water, and remove connective tissues.
3. Cut meat and offal into cubes and feed them through a meat grinder. Cook in water (slightly covering the meat).
4. Dice carrot and blueberries into tiny cubes and add it to the mixture.
5. Cook white rice according to the label, add to the mixture so it can soak up the liquid.
6. Mix it carefully.
7. Let it cool down completely, then serve or freeze in portions.

BISON, BEETROOT & BROWN RICE

Ingredients:

- 19.4 oz bison (550 g)
- 3.5 oz offal (1.1 oz chicken liver, 0.7 oz chicken heart, 1.7 oz chicken gizzard) (100 g)
- 5.3 oz brown rice (150 g)
- 7 oz beetroot (200 g)

Nutrition Facts
(Analytical components in 100g):

- Energy   185 kcal
- Fat   9.1 g
- Carbohydrate 8 g
- Fiber   0.9 g
- Protein   17.3 g

Preparation:

1. Prepare ingredients at room temperature. Remove half the fat from the meat. Remove bones. Rinse meat carefully.
2. Clean liver, heart, and gizzard thoroughly, soak them in cold water, and remove connective tissues.
3. Cut meat and offal into cubes and feed them through a meat grinder. Cook in water (slightly covering the meat).
4. Dice beetroot into tiny cubes and add it to the mixture.
5. Cook brown rice according to the label, add to the mixture so it can soak up the liquid.
6. Mix it carefully.
7. Let it cool down completely, then serve or freeze in portions.

BISON, CARROT & WHITE RICE

Ingredients:

- 19.4 oz bison (550 g)
- 3.5 oz offal (1.1 oz chicken liver, 0.7 oz chicken heart, 1.7 oz chicken gizzard) (100 g)
- 5.3 oz white rice (150 g)
- 7 oz carrot (200 g)

Preparation:

1. Prepare ingredients at room temperature. Remove half the fat from the meat. Remove bones. Rinse meat carefully.
2. Clean liver, heart, and gizzard thoroughly, soak them in cold water, and remove connective tissues.
3. Cut meat and offal into cubes and feed them through a meat grinder. Cook in water (slightly covering the meat).
4. Dice carrot into tiny cubes and add it to the mixture.
5. Cook white rice according to the label, add to the mixture so it can soak up the liquid.
6. Mix it carefully.
7. Let it cool down completely, then serve or freeze in portions.

Nutrition Facts
(Analytical components in 100g):

- Energy   188 kcal
- Fat   9.1 g
- Carbohydrate   8.7 g
- Fiber   0.7 g
- Protein   16.9 g

BEEF, BISON, EGG & BARLEY

Ingredients:

- 14 oz beef (400 g)
- 5.3 oz bison (150 g)
- 3.5 oz offal (1.7 oz beef liver, 1.8 oz beef heart) (100 g)
- 3.5 oz barley (100 g)
- 7 oz carrot (200 g)
- 1 egg

Preparation:

1. Prepare ingredients at room temperature. Remove half the fat from the meat. Remove bones. Rinse meat carefully.
2. Clean liver, heart, and gizzard thoroughly, soak them in cold water, and remove connective tissues.
3. Cut meat and offal into cubes and feed them through a meat grinder. Cook in water (slightly covering the meat).
4. Dice carrot into tiny cubes and add it to the mixture. Add egg.
5. Cook barley according to the label, add to the mixture so it can soak up the liquid.
6. Mix it carefully.
7. Let it cool down completely, then serve or freeze in portions.

Nutrition Facts
(Analytical components in 100g):

- Energy   252 kcal
- Fat   12.9 g
- Carbohydrate   7.7 g
- Fiber   1.2 g
- Protein   25.7 g

BEEF, BISON & BARLEY

Ingredients:

- 14 oz beef (400 g)
- 5.3 oz bison (150 g)
- 3.5 oz offal (1.7 oz beef liver, 1.8 oz beef heart) (100 g)
- 5.3 oz barley (150 g)
- 7 oz beetroot (200 g)

Nutrition Facts
(Analytical components in 100g):

- Energy   179 kcal
- Fat   8.1 g
- Carbohydrate   7.1 g
- Fiber   1 g
- Protein   19.6 g

Preparation:

1. Prepare ingredients at room temperature. Remove half the fat from the meat. Remove bones. Rinse meat carefully.
2. Clean liver, heart, and gizzard thoroughly, soak them in cold water, and remove connective tissues.
3. Cut meat and offal into cubes and feed them through a meat grinder. Cook in water (slightly covering the meat).
4. Dice beetroot into tiny cubes and add it to the mixture.
5. Cook barley according to the label, add to the mixture so it can soak up the liquid.
6. Mix it carefully.
7. Let it cool down completely, then serve or freeze in portions.

BEEF, KANGAROO & BARLEY

Ingredients:

- 14 oz beef (400 g)
- 5.3 oz kangaroo (150 g)
- 3.5 oz offal (1.7 oz beef liver, 1.8 oz beef heart) (100 g)
- 5.3 oz barley (150 g)
- 7 oz carrot (200 g)
- 1 egg

Nutrition Facts
(Analytical components in 100g):

- Energy   164 kcal
- Fat   6.2 g
- Carbohydrate   7.3 g
- Fiber   1.2 g
- Protein   19.6 g

Preparation:

1. Prepare ingredients at room temperature. Remove half the fat from the meat. Remove bones. Rinse meat carefully.
2. Clean liver, heart, and gizzard thoroughly, soak them in cold water, and remove connective tissues.
3. Cut meat and offal into cubes and feed them through a meat grinder. Cook in water (slightly covering the meat).
4. Dice carrot into tiny cubes and add it to the mixture. Add egg.
5. Cook barley according to the label, add to the mixture so it can soak up the liquid.
6. Mix it carefully.
7. Let it cool down completely, then serve or freeze in portions.

BEEF, KANGAROO & WHITE RICE

Ingredients:

- 14 oz beef (400 g)
- 5.3 oz kangaroo (150 g)
- 3.5 oz offal (1.7 oz beef liver, 1.8 oz beef heart) (100 g)
- 5.3 oz white rice (150 g)
- 7 oz beetroot (200 g)
- 1 egg

Preparation:

1. Prepare ingredients at room temperature. Remove half the fat from the meat. Remove bones. Rinse meat carefully.
2. Clean liver, heart, and gizzard thoroughly, soak them in cold water, and remove connective tissues.
3. Cut meat and offal into cubes and feed them through a meat grinder. Cook in water (slightly covering the meat).
4. Dice beetroot into tiny cubes and add it to the mixture. Add egg.
5. Cook white rice according to the label, add to the mixture so it can soak up the liquid.
6. Mix it carefully.
7. Let it cool down completely, then serve or freeze in portions.

Nutrition Facts
(Analytical components in 100g):

- Energy   161 kcal
- Fat   6.2 g
- Carbohydrate   6.3 g
- Fiber   1.2 g
- Protein   18.6 g

GOAT, CHICKEN & WHITE RICE

Ingredients:

- 14 oz goat (400 g)
- 10.6 oz chicken breast (300 g)
- 3.5 oz offal (1.7 oz venison liver, 1.8 oz venison heart) (100 g)
- 5.3 oz white rice (150 g)
- 3.5 oz beetroot (100 g)

Preparation:

1. Prepare ingredients at room temperature. Remove half the fat from meat. Remove bones. Rinse meat carefully.
2. Clean liver, heart, and gizzard thoroughly, soak them in cold water, and remove connective tissues.
3. Cut meat and offal into cubes and feed them through a meat grinder. Cook in water (slightly covering the meat).
4. Dice beetroot into tiny cubes and add it to the mixture.
5. Cook white rice according to the label, add to the mixture so it can soak up the liquid.
6. Mix it carefully.
7. Let it cool down completely, then serve or freeze in portions.

Nutrition Facts
(Analytical components in 100g):

- Energy   121 kcal
- Fat   3.9 g
- Carbohydrate   4.8 g
- Fiber   0.8 g
- Protein   13.5 g

CHICKEN, SARDINE & BROWN RICE

Ingredients:

- 14 oz chicken thighs (400 g)
- 5.3 oz sardine (canned) (150 g)
- 3.5 oz offal (1.1 oz chicken liver, 0.7 oz chicken heart, 1.7 oz chicken gizzard) (100 g)
- 5.3 oz brown rice (150 g)
- 7 oz sweet potato (200 g)

Preparation:

1. Prepare ingredients at room temperature. Remove half the skin and fat from the thighs. Remove bones. Rinse meat carefully.
2. Clean liver, heart, and gizzard thoroughly, soak them in cold water, and remove connective tissues.
3. Cut thighs and offal into cubes and feed them through a meat grinder. Cook in water (slightly covering the meat).
4. Dice sweet potato into tiny cubes and add it to the mixture. Add sardine.
5. Cook brown rice according to the label, add to the mixture so it can soak up the liquid.
6. Mix it carefully.
7. Let it cool down completely, then serve or freeze in portions.

Nutrition Facts
(Analytical components in 100g):

- Energy   181 kcal
- Fat   8.3 g
- Carbohydrate   9.8 g
- Fiber   1.1 g
- Protein   18 g

TURKEY, CHICKEN & MILLET

Ingredients:

- 10.6 oz turkey (300 g)
- 5.3 oz chicken breast (150 g)
- 3.5 oz offal (1.1 oz chicken liver, 0.7 oz chicken heart, 1.7 oz chicken gizzard) (100 g)
- 5.3 oz millet (150 g)
- 7 oz beetroot (200 g)
- 3.5 oz carrot (100 g)

Preparation:

1. Prepare ingredients at room temperature. Remove all the skin and fat from the thighs and breast. Remove bones. Rinse meat carefully.
2. Clean liver, heart, and gizzard thoroughly, soak them in cold water, and remove connective tissues.
3. Cut thighs, breast, offal into cubes and feed them through a meat grinder. Cook in water (slightly covering the meat).
4. Dice beetroot and carrot into tiny cubes and add it to the mixture.
5. Cook millet according to the label, add to the mixture so it can soak up the liquid.
6. Mix it carefully.
7. Let it cool down completely, then serve or freeze in portions.

Nutrition Facts
(Analytical components in 100g):

- Energy   122 kcal
- Fat   2.8 g
- Carbohydrate   5.8 g
- Fiber   0.4 g
- Protein   22.6 g

TURKEY, BEEF & BARLEY

Ingredients:

- 10.6 oz turkey (300 g)
- 5.3 oz beef (150 g)
- 3.5 oz offal (1.1 oz chicken liver, 0.7 oz chicken heart, 1.7 oz chicken gizzard) (100 g)
- 5.3 oz barley (150 g)
- 7 oz pumpkin (200 g)
- 3.5 oz broccoli (100 g)

Nutrition Facts
(Analytical components in 100g):

- Energy — 129 kcal
- Fat — 3.8 g
- Carbohydrate — 5.7 g
- Fiber — 0.7 g
- Protein — 24.6 g

Preparation:

1. Prepare ingredients at room temperature. Remove all the skin and fat from the meat. Remove bones. Rinse meat carefully.
2. Clean liver, heart, and gizzard thoroughly, soak them in cold water, and remove connective tissues.
3. Cut meat and offal into cubes and feed them through a meat grinder. Cook in water (slightly covering the meat).
4. Dice pumpkin and broccoli into tiny cubes and add it to the mixture.
5. Cook barley according to the label, add to the mixture so it can soak up the liquid.
6. Mix it carefully.
7. Let it cool down completely, then serve or freeze in portions.

DUCK, BEEF & MILLET

Ingredients:

- 12.3 oz duck (350 g)
- 3.5 oz offal (1.7 oz duck liver, 1.8 oz duck heart) (100 g)
- 10.6 oz beef (lean) (300 g)
- 3.5 oz millet (100 g)
- 3.5 oz pumpkin (100 g)
- 1.7 oz broccoli (50 g)

Nutrition Facts
(Analytical components in 100g):

- Energy — 230 kcal
- Fat — 14.9 g
- Carbohydrate — 5.2 g
- Fiber — 0.4 g
- Protein — 14.6 g

Preparation:

1. Prepare ingredients at room temperature. Rinse meat carefully.
2. Clean liver and heart thoroughly, soak them in cold water, and remove connective tissues.
3. Cut meat and offal into cubes and feed them through a meat grinder (optionally you can feed meat in bigger chunks, too). Cook in water (slightly covering the meat).
4. Cook millet according to the packaging label, add to the mixture to soak up liquid.
5. Dice pumpkin and broccoli into tiny cubes, and add it to the mixture.
6. Mix it carefully.
7. Freeze in portions.

PORK, SARDINE & BROWN RICE

Ingredients:
- 12.3 oz pork (350 g)
- 150 g sardine (canned) (150 g)
- 3.5 oz offal (1.1 oz chicken liver, 0.7 oz chicken heart, 1.7 oz chicken gizzard) (100 g)
- 7 oz brown rice (200 g)
- 7 oz sweet potato (200 g)

Preparation:
1. Prepare ingredients at room temperature. Remove half the fat from the meat. Remove bones. Rinse meat carefully.
2. Clean liver, heart, and gizzard thoroughly, soak them in cold water, and remove connective tissues.
3. Cut meat and offal into cubes and feed them through a meat grinder. Cook in water (slightly covering the meat).
4. Cook brown rice according to the label, add to mixture to soak up liquid. Add sardine.
5. Dice sweet potato into tiny cubes and add it to the mixture.
6. Mix it carefully.
7. Let it cool down completely, then serve or freeze in portions.

Nutrition Facts
(Analytical components in 100g):

- Energy   174 kcal
- Fat   6.2 g
- Carbohydrate 9.8 g
- Fiber   1.1 g
- Protein   19.1 g

PORK & GRAINS

Ingredients:
- 17.6 oz pork (500 g)
- 3.5 oz offal (1.1 oz chicken liver, 0.7 oz chicken heart, 1.7 oz chicken gizzard) (100 g)
- 7 oz brown rice (200 g)
- 3.5 oz millet (100 g)
- 3.5 oz sweet potato (100 g)

Preparation:
1. Prepare ingredients at room temperature. Remove half the fat from the meat. Remove bones. Rinse meat carefully.
2. Clean liver, heart, and gizzard thoroughly, soak them in cold water, and remove connective tissues.
3. Cut meat and offal into cubes and feed them through a meat grinder. Cook in water (slightly covering the meat).
4. Cook grains according to the label, add to mixture to soak up liquid.
5. Dice sweet potato into tiny cubes and add it to the mixture.
6. Mix it carefully.
7. Let it cool down completely, then serve or freeze in portions.

Nutrition Facts
(Analytical components in 100g):

- Energy   155 kcal
- Fat   4.8 g
- Carbohydrate 13.1 g
- Fiber   1.2 g
- Protein   15 g

PORK, SALMON & RICE

Ingredients:

- 550 g pork (550 g)
- 3.5 oz offal (1.7 oz lamb liver, 1.8 oz lamb heart) (100 g)
- 3.5 oz white rice (100 g)
- 5.3 oz salmon (boneless) (150 g)
- 3.5 oz carrot (100 g)

Nutrition Facts
(Analytical components in 100g):

- Energy   148 kcal
- Fat   6.4 g
- Carbohydrate 4.4 g
- Fiber   0.3 g
- Protein   17.9 g

Preparation:

1. Prepare ingredients at room temperature. Rinse meat carefully.
2. Clean liver and heart thoroughly, soak them in cold water, and remove connective tissues.
3. Cut pork, salmon, and offal into cubes and feed them through a meat grinder (optionally you can feed meat in bigger chunks, too). Cook in water (slightly covering the meat).
4. Cook white rice according to the packaging label. Add to mixture to soak up liquid.
5. Dice carrot into tiny cubes, and add it to the mixture.
6. Mix it carefully.
7. Freeze in portions.

CHICKEN, KANGAROO & BROWN RICE

Ingredients:

- 7 oz chicken breast (200 g)
- 12.3 oz kangaroo (350 g)
- 3.5 oz offal (1.1 oz chicken liver, 0.7 oz chicken heart, 1.8 oz chicken gizzard) (100 g)
- 7 oz brown rice (200 G)
- 3.5 oz carrot (100 g)
- 1.7 oz blueberries (50g)

Nutrition Facts
(Analytical components in 100g):

- Energy   138 kcal
- Fat   3.3 g
- Carbohydrate 7.9 g
- Fiber   1.2 g
- Protein   21.8 g

Preparation:

1. Prepare ingredients at room temperature. Remove half the skin and fat from the breast. Remove bones. Rinse meat carefully.
2. Clean liver, heart, and gizzard thoroughly, soak them in cold water, and remove connective tissues.
3. Cut meat and offal into cubes and feed them through a meat grinder. Cook in water (slightly covering the meat).
4. Dice carrot and blueberries into tiny cubes and add it to the mixture.
5. Cook brown rice according to the label, add to the mixture so it can soak up the liquid.
6. Mix it carefully.
7. Let it cool down completely, then serve or freeze in portions.

OSTRICH, BEETROOT & BROWN RICE

Ingredients:

- 19.4 oz ostrich (550 g)
- 3.5 oz offal (1.1 oz chicken liver, 0.7 oz chicken heart, 1.7 oz chicken gizzard) (100 g)
- 5.3 oz brown rice (150 g)
- 7 oz beetroot (200 g)

Preparation:

1. Prepare ingredients at room temperature. Remove half the skin and fat from the meat. Remove bones if you're going to bake the loaf. Rinse meat carefully.
2. Clean liver, heart, and gizzard thoroughly, soak them in cold water, and remove connective tissues.
3. Cut meat and offal into cubes and feed them through a meat grinder. Cook in water (slightly covering the meat).
4. Dice beetroot into tiny cubes and add it to the mixture.
5. Cook brown rice according to the label, add to the mixture so it can soak up the liquid.
6. Mix it carefully.
7. Let it cool down completely, then serve or freeze in portions.

Nutrition Facts
(Analytical components in 100g):

- Energy   138 kcal
- Fat   2.9 g
- Carbohydrate   8 g
- Fiber   0.9 g
- Protein   20.6 g

OSTRICH, CHICKEN & MILLET

Ingredients:

- 14 oz ostrich (400 g)
- 5.3 oz chicken breast (150 g)
- 3.5 oz offal (1.1 oz chicken liver, 0.7 oz chicken heart, 1.7 oz chicken gizzard) (100 g)
- 5.3 oz millet (150 g)
- 7 oz beetroot (200 g)

Preparation:

1. Prepare ingredients at room temperature. Remove half the skin and fat from the meat. Remove bones if you're going to bake the loaf. Rinse meat carefully.
2. Clean liver, heart, and gizzard thoroughly, soak them in cold water, and remove connective tissues.
3. Cut meat and offal into cubes and feed them through a meat grinder. Cook in water (slightly covering the meat).
4. Dice beetroot into tiny cubes and add it to the mixture.
5. Cook millet according to the label, add to the mixture so it can soak up the liquid.
6. Mix it carefully.
7. Let it cool down completely, then serve or freeze in portions.

Nutrition Facts
(Analytical components in 100g):

- Energy   138 kcal
- Fat   2.9 g
- Carbohydrate   8 g
- Fiber   0.9 g
- Protein   20.6 g

OSTRICH, SALMON & BROWN RICE

Ingredients:

- 14 oz ostrich (400 g)
- 5.3 oz salmon (150 g)
- 3.5 oz offal (1.1 oz chicken liver, 0.7 oz chicken heart, 1.7 oz chicken gizzard) (100 g)
- 5.3 oz brown rice (150 g)
- 7 oz beetroot (200 g)

Nutrition Facts
(Analytical components in 100g):

- Energy   138 kcal
- Fat   4.9 g
- Carbohydrate   8 g
- Fiber   0.9 g
- Protein   19.6 g

Preparation:

1. Prepare ingredients at room temperature. Remove half the skin and fat from the meat. Remove bones if you're going to bake the loaf. Rinse meat carefully.
2. Clean liver, heart, and gizzard thoroughly, soak them in cold water, and remove connective tissues.
3. Cut meat and offal into cubes and feed them through a meat grinder. Cook in water (slightly covering the meat).
4. Dice beetroot into tiny cubes and add it to the mixture.
5. Cook brown rice according to the label, add to the mixture so it can soak up the liquid.
6. Mix it carefully.
7. Let it cool down completely, then serve or freeze in portions.

OSTRICH, BEEF & BROWN RICE

Ingredients:

- 14 oz ostrich (400 g)
- 5.3 oz beef (lean) (150 g)
- 3.5 oz offal (1.1 oz chicken liver, 0.7 oz chicken heart, 1.7 oz chicken gizzard) (100 g)
- 5.3 oz brown rice (150 g)
- 7 oz beetroot (200 g)

Nutrition Facts
(Analytical components in 100g):

- Energy   144 kcal
- Fat   4.9 g
- Carbohydrate   8 g
- Fiber   0.9 g
- Protein   23.6 g

Preparation:

1. Prepare ingredients at room temperature. Remove half the skin and fat from the meat. Remove bones if you're going to bake the loaf. Rinse meat carefully.
2. Clean liver, heart, and gizzard thoroughly, soak them in cold water, and remove connective tissues.
3. Cut meat and offal into cubes and feed them through a meat grinder. Cook in water (slightly covering the meat).
4. Dice beetroot into tiny cubes and add it to the mixture.
5. Cook brown rice according to the label, add to the mixture so it can soak up the liquid.
6. Mix it carefully.
7. Let it cool down completely, then serve or freeze in portions.

OSTRICH, LAMB & BROWN RICE

Ingredients:

- 14 oz ostrich (400 g)
- 5.3 oz lamb (150 g)
- 3.5 oz offal (1.1 oz chicken liver, 0.7 oz chicken heart, 1.7 oz chicken gizzard) (100 g)
- 5.3 oz brown rice (150 g)
- 7 oz sweet potato (200 g)

Nutrition Facts
(Analytical components in 100g):

- Energy   124 kcal
- Fat   2.1 g
- Carbohydrate   8 g
- Fiber   0.7 g
- Protein   21.8 g

Preparation:

1. Prepare ingredients at room temperature. Remove half the skin and fat from the meat. Remove bones if you're going to bake the loaf. Rinse meat carefully.
2. Clean liver, heart, and gizzard thoroughly, soak them in cold water, and remove connective tissues.
3. Cut meat and offal into cubes and feed them through a meat grinder. Cook in water (slightly covering the meat).
4. Dice sweet potato into tiny cubes and add it to the mixture.
5. Cook brown rice according to the label, add to the mixture so it can soak up the liquid.
6. Mix it carefully.
7. Let it cool down completely, then serve or freeze in portions.

CHICKEN, VENISON & WHITE RICE

Ingredients:

- 14 oz chicken breast (400 g)
- 10.6 oz venison (300 g)
- 3.5 oz offal (1.7 oz venison liver, 1.8 oz venison heart) (100 g)
- 3.5 oz white rice (100 g)
- 3.5 oz beetroot (100 g)

Nutrition Facts
(Analytical components in 100g):

- Energy   124 kcal
- Fat   2.4 g
- Carbohydrate   6.7 g
- Fiber   0.6 g
- Protein   21.1 g

Preparation:

1. Prepare ingredients at room temperature. Rinse meat carefully.
2. Clean liver and heart thoroughly, soak them in cold water, and remove connective tissues.
3. Cut meat and offal into cubes and feed them through a meat grinder (optionally you can feed meat in bigger chunks, too). Cook in water (slightly covering the meat).
4. Cook white rice according to the packaging label, add to soak up liquid.
5. Dice beetroot into tiny cubes, and add it to the mixture.
6. Mix it carefully.
7. Freeze in portions.

BEEF, VENISON & WHITE RICE

Ingredients:

- 14 oz beef (400 g)
- 10.6 oz venison (300 g)
- 3.5 oz offal (1.7 oz venison liver, 1.8 oz venison heart) (100 g)
- 3.5 oz white rice (100 g)
- 3.5 oz beetroot (100 g)

Preparation:

1. Prepare ingredients at room temperature. Rinse meat carefully.
2. Clean liver and heart thoroughly, soak them in cold water, and remove connective tissues.
3. Cut meat and offal into cubes and feed them through a meat grinder (optionally you can feed meat in bigger chunks, too). Cook in water (slightly covering the meat).
4. Cook white rice according to the packaging label, add to soak up liquid.
5. Dice beetroot into tiny cubes, and add it to the mixture.
6. Mix it carefully.
7. Freeze in portions.

Nutrition Facts
(Analytical components in 100g):

- Energy   137 kcal
- Fat   3.4 g
- Carbohydrate   6.7 g
- Fiber   0.6 g
- Protein   24.1 g

DUCK, VENISON & MILLET

Ingredients:

- 12.3 oz duck (350 g)
- 3.5 oz offal (1.7 oz duck liver, 1.8 oz duck heart) (100 g)
- 10.6 oz venison (300 g)
- 3.5 oz millet (100 g)
- 3.5 oz carrot (100 g)
- 1.7 oz broccoli (50 g)

Preparation:

1. Prepare ingredients at room temperature. Rinse meat carefully.
2. Clean liver and heart thoroughly, soak them in cold water, and remove connective tissues.
3. Cut meat and offal into cubes and feed them through a meat grinder (optionally you can feed meat in bigger chunks, too). Cook in water (slightly covering the meat).
4. Cook millet according to the packaging label.
5. Dice carrot and broccoli into tiny cubes, and add it to the mixture.
6. Mix it carefully.
7. Freeze in portions.

Nutrition Facts
(Analytical components in 100g):

- Energy   253 kcal
- Fat   18.9 g
- Carbohydrate   5.3 g
- Fiber   0.2 g
- Protein   18.6 g

CHICKEN, APPLE & WHITE RICE

Ingredients:

- 14 oz chicken breast (400 g)
- 3.5 oz offal (1.1 oz chicken liver, 0.7 oz chicken heart, 1.7 oz chicken gizzard) (100 g)
- 10.6 oz white rice (300 g)
- 3.5 oz carrot (100 g)
- 3.5 oz apple (100 g)

Nutrition Facts
(Analytical components in 100g):

- Energy   121 kcal
- Fat   1.1 g
- Carbohydrate   9.5 g
- Fiber   0.9 g
- Protein   17.6 g

Preparation:

1. Prepare ingredients at room temperature. Remove half the skin and fat from the meat. Remove bones if you're going to bake the loaf. Rinse meat carefully.
2. Clean liver, heart, and gizzard thoroughly, soak them in cold water, and remove connective tissues.
3. Cut meat and offal into cubes and feed them through a meat grinder. Cook in water (slightly covering the meat)
4. Cook rice according to the packaging label, add to mixture to soak up the liquid.
5. Dice carrot and apple into tiny cubes and add it to the mixture.
6. Mix it carefully.
7. Let it cool down completely, then serve or freeze in portions.

BEEF, APPLE & BROWN RICE

Ingredients:

- 14 oz beef (400 g)
- 3.5 oz offal (1.1 oz chicken liver, 0.7 oz chicken heart, 1.7 oz chicken gizzard) (100 g)
- 10.6 oz brown rice (300 g)
- 3.5 oz carrot (100 g)
- 3.5 oz apple (100 g)

Nutrition Facts
(Analytical components in 100g):

- Energy   132 kcal
- Fat   1.8 g
- Carbohydrate   9.5 g
- Fiber   0.9 g
- Protein   19.6 g

Preparation:

1. Prepare ingredients at room temperature. Remove half the skin and fat from the meat. Remove bones if you're going to bake the loaf. Rinse meat carefully.
2. Clean liver, heart, and gizzard thoroughly, soak them in cold water, and remove connective tissues.
3. Cut meat and offal into cubes and feed them through a meat grinder. Cook in water (slightly covering the meat)
4. Cook brown rice according to the packaging label, add to mixture to soak up the liquid.
5. Dice carrot and apple into tiny cubes and add it to the mixture.
6. Mix it carefully.
7. Let it cool down completely, then serve or freeze in portions.

LAMB, APPLE & WHITE RICE

Ingredients:

- 14 oz lamb (400 g)
- 3.5 oz offal (1.1 oz chicken liver, 0.7 oz chicken heart, 1.7 oz chicken gizzard) (100 g)
- 10.6 oz white rice (300 g)
- 3.5 oz carrot (100 g)
- 3.5 oz apple (100 g)

Nutrition Facts
(Analytical components in 100g):

- Energy   118 kcal
- Fat   1.4 g
- Carbohydrate   9.5 g
- Fiber   0.9 g
- Protein   15.6 g

Preparation:

1. Prepare ingredients at room temperature. Remove half the fat from the meat. Remove bones if you're going to bake the loaf. Rinse meat carefully.
2. Clean liver, heart, and gizzard thoroughly, soak them in cold water, and remove connective tissues.
3. Cut meat and offal into cubes and feed them through a meat grinder. Cook in water (slightly covering the meat).
4. Cook rice according to the packaging label, add to mixture to soak up the liquid.
5. Dice carrot and apple into tiny cubes and add it to the mixture.
6. Mix it carefully.
7. Let it cool down completely, then serve or freeze in portions.

BISON, APPLE & WHITE RICE

Ingredients:

- 14 oz bison (400 g)
- 3.5 oz offal (1.1 oz chicken liver, 0.7 oz chicken heart, 1.7 oz chicken gizzard) (100 g)
- 10.6 oz white rice (300 g)
- 3.5 oz carrot (100 g)
- 3.5 oz apple (100 g)

Nutrition Facts
(Analytical components in 100g):

- Energy   133 kcal
- Fat   1.6 g
- Carbohydrate   9.5 g
- Fiber   0.9 g
- Protein   18.9 g

Preparation:

1. Prepare ingredients at room temperature. Remove half the fat from the meat. Remove bones if you're going to bake the loaf. Rinse meat carefully.
2. Clean liver, heart, and gizzard thoroughly, soak them in cold water, and remove connective tissues.
3. Cut meat and offal into cubes and feed them through a meat grinder. Cook in water (slightly covering the meat).
4. Cook rice according to the packaging label, add to mixture to soak up the liquid.
5. Dice carrot and apple into tiny cubes and add it to the mixture.
6. Mix it carefully.
7. Let it cool down completely, then serve or freeze in portions.

GOAT, BEEF & BROWN RICE

Ingredients:

- 14 oz goat (400 g)
- 10.6 oz beef (300 g)
- 3.5 oz offal (1.7 oz venison liver, 1.8 oz venison heart) (100 g)
- 3.5 oz brown rice (100 g)
- 3.5 oz beetroot (100 g)

Preparation:

1. Prepare ingredients at room temperature. Rinse meat carefully.
2. Clean liver and heart thoroughly, soak them in cold water, and remove connective tissues.
3. Cut meat and offal into cubes and feed them through a meat grinder (optionally you can feed meat in bigger chunks, too). Cook in water (slightly covering the meat).
4. Cook brown rice according to the packaging label.
5. Dice beetroot into tiny cubes, and add it to the mixture.
6. Mix it carefully.
7. Freeze in portions.

Nutrition Facts
(Analytical components in 100g):

- Energy   132 kcal
- Fat   2.9 g
- Carbohydrate   6.3 g
- Fiber   0.8 g
- Protein   24.3 g

GOAT, LAMB & BROWN RICE

Ingredients:

- 14 oz goat (400 g)
- 10.6 oz lamb (300 g)
- 3.5 oz offal (1.7 oz venison liver, 1.8 oz venison heart) (100 g)
- 3.5 oz brown rice (100 g)
- 3.5 oz pumpkin (100 g)

Preparation:

1. Prepare ingredients at room temperature. Rinse meat carefully.
2. Clean liver and heart thoroughly, soak them in cold water, and remove connective tissues.
3. Cut meat and offal into cubes and feed them through a meat grinder (optionally you can feed meat in bigger chunks, too). Cook in water (slightly covering the meat).
4. Cook brown rice according to the packaging label.
5. Dice pumpkin into tiny cubes, and add it to the mixture.
6. Mix it carefully.
7. Freeze in portions.

Nutrition Facts
(Analytical components in 100g):

- Energy   131 kcal
- Fat   2.3 g
- Carbohydrate   6.3 g
- Fiber   0.8 g
- Protein   22.7 g

GOAT, SALMON & BUCKWHEAT

Ingredients:

- 14 oz goat (400 g)
- 10.6 oz salmon (boneless) (300 g)
- 3.5 oz offal (1.7 oz venison liver, 1.8 oz venison heart) (100 g)
- 3.5 oz buckwheat (100 g)
- 3.5 oz pumpkin (100 g)

Nutrition Facts
(Analytical components in 100g):

- Energy   128 kcal
- Fat   2.2 g
- Carbohydrate   6.1 g
- Fiber   0.8 g
- Protein   18.3 g

Preparation:

1. Prepare ingredients at room temperature. Rinse meat carefully.
2. Clean liver and heart thoroughly, soak them in cold water, and remove connective tissues.
3. Cut meat, salmon and offal into cubes and feed them through a meat grinder (optionally you can feed meat in bigger chunks, too). Cook in water (slightly covering the meat).
4. Cook buckwheat according to the packaging label.
5. Dice pumpkin into tiny cubes, and add it to the mixture.
6. Mix it carefully.
7. Freeze in portions.

GOAT, RABBIT & WHITE RICE

Ingredients:

- 14 oz goat (400 g)
- 300 g rabbit (300 g)
- 3.5 oz offal (1.7 oz venison liver, 1.8 oz venison heart) (100 g)
- 3.5 oz white rice (100 g)
- 3.5 oz carrot (100 g)

Nutrition Facts
(Analytical components in 100g):

- Energy   123 kcal
- Fat   2.1 g
- Carbohydrate   6.7 g
- Fiber   0.6 g
- Protein   19.2 g

Preparation:

1. Prepare ingredients at room temperature. Rinse meat carefully.
2. Clean liver and heart thoroughly, soak them in cold water, and remove connective tissues.
3. Cut meat and offal into cubes and feed them through a meat grinder (optionally you can feed meat in bigger chunks, too). Cook in water (slightly covering the meat).
4. Cook white rice according to the packaging label, add to soak up liquid.
5. Dice carrot into tiny cubes, and add it to the mixture.
6. Mix it carefully.
7. Freeze in portions.

LEAN KANGAROO, CARROT & WHITE RICE

Ingredients:

- 500 g kangaroo (500 g)
- 3.5 oz offal (1.1 oz chicken liver, 0.7 oz chicken heart, 1.7 oz chicken gizzard) (100 g)
- 7 oz white rice (200 g)
- 7 oz carrot (200 g)

Nutrition Facts
(Analytical components in 100g):

- Energy   122 kcal
- Fat   3.3 g
- Carbohydrate   7.2 g
- Fiber   0.9 g
- Protein   19.4 g

Preparation:

1. Prepare ingredients at room temperature. Remove half the fat from the meat. Remove bones. Rinse meat carefully.
2. Clean liver, heart, and gizzard thoroughly, soak them in cold water, and remove connective tissues.
3. Cut meat and offal into cubes and feed them through a meat grinder. Cook in water (slightly covering the meat).
4. Dice carrot into tiny cubes and add it to the mixture.
5. Cook white rice according to the label, add to the mixture so it can soak up the liquid.
6. Mix it carefully.
7. Let it cool down completely, then serve or freeze in portions.

KIBBLE

In this section you will find easy-to-make dry kibble that you can prepare at home. And the best thing is: you know all the ingredients that go into your dog's food bowl.

TO MAKE CORRECT PORTIONS:
Every recipe provided in this section is well-balanced, and you will always find the nutritional analysis at the end. However, the most important factor to consider is the calorie intake because based on that, you can easily calculate the correct daily portion for your dog.

Let's take an example: if your dog has a daily energy requirement (DER) of 630 kcal/day and the recipe you are preparing contains 148 kcal per 100 g, you can use this simple formula to determine the appropriate portion:

$$\text{Daily Meal Portion (g)} = 100 \times \text{DER} / \text{Meal kcal}$$

e.g., Daily Meal Portion (g) = 100 x 630 / 148 = 425 g (15 oz)

Remember that **knowing your dog's calorie requirement is essential to help them maintain their ideal weight.** You can use the information found in this book, specifically in the chapter titled "Feeding Guidelines & Calorie Calculation," or seek assistance from a veterinarian for added assurance.

VEGGIE LOVER KIBBLE

Ingredients:

- 10.6 oz brown rice (300 g)
- 5 cup water (1200 g)
- 3.5 oz carrot (100 g)
- 3.5 oz sweet potato (100 g)
- 5.3 oz beetroot (150 g)
- 1.7 oz broccoli (50 g)
- 1.1 oz coconut oil (30 g)

Nutrition Facts
(Analytical components in 100g):

- Energy   112 kcal
- Fat   2.6 g
- Carbohydrate   21.2 g
- Fiber   1.9 g
- Protein   2.2 g

Preparation:

1. Preheat oven to 338 F (170° C)
2. Prepare ingredients at room temperature.
3. Cook brown rice in water according to the packaging label.
4. Cut carrot, sweet potato, beetroot, and broccoli into tiny cubes.
5. Add veggies to brown rice, let it steam for a while, and then add coconut oil.
6. Put the mixture into a food processor and mix until you get a homogenous puree. Adjust amounts if necessary.
7. Spread the mixture on a baking tray (maximum 5mm thin layer) lined with parchment paper.
8. Bake it for 35-40 minutes, then turn the batter over and bake for another 30 minutes to make sure it completely dries out. Take it out and let it rest.
9. Reduce oven temperature to 284 F (140° C). Cut batter into smaller pieces, put the pieces back onto the baking tray, and bake for another 45-50 minutes until golden brown.
10. Let it cool down, and break or cut to desired size.
11. Kibble can be stored in the fridge for 7-8 days.

BEEF & BLUEBERRY KIBBLE

Ingredients:

- 12.3 oz oat flour (350 g)
- 3.5 oz beef (boneless) (100 g)
- 2 large eggs
- 5.3 oz beetroot (diced) (150 g)
- 1.7 oz blueberries (50 g)
- 1.1 oz coconut oil (30 g)

Nutrition Facts
(Analytical components in 100g):

- Energy   269 kcal
- Fat   10.5 g
- Carbohydrate   31.6 g
- Fiber   3.4 g
- Protein   12 g

Preparation:

1. Preheat oven to 338 F (170° C)
2. Prepare ingredients at room temperature.
3. Mix eggs and coconut oil with beetroot and blueberries.
4. Add oat flour to the mixture, incorporating until fully combined.
5. Cut beef into cubes and brown them in a pan until pieces cook through. Add pieces to the oat mixture.
6. Put the mixture into a food processor and mix until you get a homogenous puree. Adjust amounts if necessary. You can add water if the mix is too thick.
7. Spread the mixture on a baking tray (maximum 5mm thin layer) lined with parchment paper.
8. Bake it for 35-40 minutes until golden brown, to make sure it dries out completely. Reduce oven temperature if necessary.
9. Let it cool down on a cooling rack, and break or cut to desired size.
10. Kibble can be stored in the fridge for 7-8 days.

PUMPKIN KIBBLE

Ingredients:

- 12.3 oz oat flour (350 g)
- 3.5 oz chicken breast (boneless) (100 g)
- 2 large eggs
- 5.3 oz pumpkin (peeled & diced) (150 g)
- 1.7 oz carrot (diced) (50 g)
- 1.1 oz coconut oil (30 g)

Nutrition Facts
(Analytical components in 100g):

- Energy   233 kcal
- Fat   8.5 g
- Carbohydrate   30 g
- Fiber   3.3 g
- Protein   12.6 g

Preparation:

1. Preheat oven to 338 F (170° C)
2. Prepare ingredients at room temperature.
3. Mix eggs and coconut oil with pumpkin and carrot.
4. Add oat flour to the mixture, incorporating until fully combined.
5. Cut chicken breast into cubes and brown them in a pan until pieces cook through. Add pieces to the oat mixture.
6. Put the mixture into a food processor and mix until you get a homogenous puree. Adjust amounts if necessary. You can add water if the mix is too thick.
7. Spread the mixture on a baking tray (maximum 5mm thin layer) lined with parchment paper.
8. Bake it for 35-40 minutes until golden brown, to make sure it dries out completely. Reduce oven temperature if necessary.
9. Let it cool down on a cooling rack, and break or cut to desired size.
10. Kibble can be stored in the fridge for 7-8 days.

CARROT & SWEET POTATO KIBBLE

Ingredients:

- 12.3 oz oat flour (350 g)
- 3.5 oz chicken thighs (boneless) (100 g)
- 2 large eggs
- 5.3 oz sweet potato (diced) (150 g)
- 1.7 oz carrot (diced) (50 g)
- 1.1 oz coconut oil (30 g)

Nutrition Facts
(Analytical components in 100g):

- Energy   255 kcal
- Fat   7.3 g
- Carbohydrate   39 g
- Fiber   2.8 g
- Protein   8.7 g

Preparation:

1. Preheat oven to 338 F (170° C)
2. Prepare ingredients at room temperature.
3. Mix eggs and coconut oil with sweet potato and carrot.
4. Add brown rice flour to the mixture, incorporating until fully combined.
5. Cut chicken thighs into cubes and brown them in a pan until pieces cook through. Add pieces to the oat mixture.
6. Put the mixture into a food processor and mix until you get a homogenous puree. Adjust amounts if necessary. You can add water if the mix is too thick.
7. Spread the mixture on a baking tray (maximum 5mm thin layer) lined with parchment paper.
8. Bake it for 35-40 minutes until golden brown, to make sure it dries out completely. Reduce oven temperature if necessary.
9. Let it cool down on a cooling rack, and break or cut to desired size.
10. Kibble can be stored in the fridge for 7-8 days.

CHICKEN & APPLE KIBBLE

Ingredients:

- 12.3 oz oat flour (350 g)
- 3.5 oz chicken thighs (boneless) (100 g)
- 2 large eggs
- 5.3 oz pumpkin (peeled and diced) (150 g)
- 1.7 oz apple (diced) (50 g)
- 1.1 oz coconut oil (30 g)

Nutrition Facts
(Analytical components in 100g):

- Energy   255 kcal
- Fat   10 g
- Carbohydrate 30.5 g
- Fiber   3.2 g
- Protein   11.5 g

Preparation:

1. Preheat oven to 338 F (170° C)
2. Prepare ingredients at room temperature.
3. Mix eggs and coconut oil with pumpkin and apple.
4. Add oat flour to the mixture, mix until fully combined.
5. Cut chicken thighs into cubes and brown them in a pan until pieces cook through. Add pieces to the oat mixture.
6. Put the mixture into a food processor and mix until you get a homogenous puree. Adjust amounts if necessary. You can add water if the mix is too thick.
7. Spread the mixture on a baking tray (maximum 5mm thin layer) lined with parchment paper.
8. Bake it for 35-40 minutes until golden brown, to make sure it dries out completely. Reduce oven temperature if necessary.
9. Let it cool down on a cooling rack, and break or cut to desired size.
10. Kibble can be stored in the fridge for 7-8 days.

TREATS

Yes, dogs can enjoy homemade treats too! Snacks and small rewards to indulge and reward your furry friend safely. These delectable treats are easy to make using wholesome ingredients. You can give them in moderation to make your dog truly happy. You can also experiment with different shapes, sizes, and flavors that perfectly cater to your dog's preferences.

BANANA & PEANUT BUTTER TREAT

Ingredients:

- 1.4 oz oat flour (140 g)
- 1 medium, ripe banana
- 1.2 oz peanut butter (unsweetened, organic) (35 g)
- ¼ tsp rosehip powder (optional)

Preparation:

1. Prepare ingredients at room temperature.
2. Preheat the oven to 338 F (170° C), line the baking tray with parchment paper.
3. Peel and then dice banana into tiny cubes.
4. Add banana cubes and peanut butter to oat flour.
5. Mix the ingredients with the food blender to get a homogeneous "dough". Adjust amounts if needed.
6. Sprinkle oat flour on a rolling board and roll the mixture.
7. Cut treats with knife or cookie cutters and bake for approximately 20 minutes, until golden brown.
8. Put them on a rack to cool completely.
9. Store in an airtight container or put them in the freezer to make them last longer.

Nutrition Facts
(Analytical components in 100g):

- Energy   312 kcal
- Fat   11.2 g
- Carbohydrate   44.7 g
- Fiber   5 g
- Protein   10.6 g

PUMPKIN & OATS TREAT

Ingredients:

- 9.2 oz pumpkin puree (sugar-free, unflavored) (260 g)
- 2.1 oz peanut butter (sugar-free, organic) (60 g)
- 3 large eggs
- 27.9 oz oat flour (790 g)
- ½ tsp rosehip powder

Preparation:

1. Prepare ingredients at room temperature.
2. Preheat the oven to 338 F (170° C), line the baking tray with parchment paper.
3. Mix the ingredients with a food blender to get a homogeneous "dough". Adjust amounts if needed.
4. Cover the bowl with cling film and put the mixture in the fridge for 20-25 minutes.
5. Sprinkle oat flour on a rolling board and roll the mixture.
6. Cut treats with knife or cookie cutters and bake for approximately 20 minutes, until golden brown.
7. Put them on a rack to cool completely.
8. Store in an airtight container or put them in the freezer to make them last longer.

Nutrition Facts
(Analytical components in 100g):

- Energy   296 kcal
- Fat   9.9 g
- Carbohydrate   41.4 g
- Fiber   4.4 g
- Protein   11.8 g

SIMPLE PEANUT BUTTER TREAT

Ingredients:

- 9.2 oz oat flour (260 g)
- 2.1 oz peanut butter (sugar-free, organic) (60 g)
- 3 medium eggs
- ⅕ cup water/bone broth (50 g)

Preparation:

1. Prepare ingredients at room temperature.
2. Preheat the oven to 347 F (175° C), line the baking tray with parchment paper.
3. Mix the ingredients in a bowl to get a homogeneous "dough". Adjust amounts if needed.
4. Sprinkle oat flour on a rolling board and roll the mixture.
5. Cut treats with knife or cookie cutters, and bake for approximately 20 minutes, until golden brown.
6. Put them on a rack to cool completely.
7. Store in an airtight container or put them in the freezer to make them last longer.

Nutrition Facts
(Analytical components in 100g):

- Energy   322 kcal
- Fat   13 g
- Carbohydrate   35.6 g
- Fiber   3.9 g
- Protein   13.8 g

BEEF DOG TREAT

Ingredients:

- 7 oz ground beef (cooked) (200 g)
- 3.2 oz buckwheat (cooked) (90 g)
- 0.4 oz oat flour (10 g)
- 1 medium egg
- ¼ tsp rosehip powder (optional)

Preparation:

1. Prepare ingredients at room temperature.
2. Preheat the oven to 356 F (180° C), line the baking tray with parchment paper.
3. Mash cooked buckwheat with a fork.
4. Mix the ingredients in a bowl to get a homogeneous "dough". Adjust amounts if needed.
5. Spoon the batter into muffin tin or oven-safe silicone mold.
6. Bake for approximately 20 minutes, until golden brown.
7. Put them on a rack to cool completely.
8. Store in an airtight container or put them in the freezer to make them last longer.

Nutrition Facts
(Analytical components in 100g):

- Energy   302 kcal
- Fat   11.2 g
- Carbohydrate   7.1 g
- Fiber   0.9 g
- Protein   18 g

LAMB DOG TREAT

Ingredients:

- 7 oz ground lamb (cooked) (200 g)
- 3.2 oz buckwheat (cooked) (90 g)
- 0.4 oz oat flour (10 g)
- 1 medium egg
- ¼ tsp rosehip powder (optional)

Preparation:

1. Prepare ingredients at room temperature.
2. Preheat the oven to 356 F (180° C), line the baking tray with parchment paper.
3. Mash cooked buckwheat with a fork.
4. Mix the ingredients in a bowl to get a homogeneous "dough". Adjust amounts if needed.
5. Spoon the batter into muffin tin or oven-safe silicone mold.
6. Bake for approximately 20 minutes, until golden brown.
7. Put them on a rack to cool completely.
8. Store in an airtight container or put them in the freezer to make them last longer.

Nutrition Facts
(Analytical components in 100g):

- Energy   222 kcal
- Fat   13.9 g
- Carbohydrate 7.1 g
- Fiber   0.9 g
- Protein   16.4 g

SALMON DOG TREAT

Ingredients:

- 7 oz ground salmon (cooked) (200 g)
- 3.2 oz buckwheat (cooked) (90 g)
- 0.4 oz oat flour (10 g)
- 1 medium egg
- ¼ tsp rosehip powder (optional)

Preparation:

1. Prepare ingredients at room temperature.
2. Preheat the oven to 356 F (180° C), line the baking tray with parchment paper.
3. Mash cooked buckwheat with a fork.
4. Mix the ingredients in a bowl to get a homogeneous "dough". Adjust amounts if needed.
5. Spoon the batter into muffin tin or oven-safe silicone mold.
6. Bake for approximately 20 minutes, until golden brown.
7. Put them on a rack to cool completely.
8. Store in an airtight container or put them in the freezer to make them last longer.

Nutrition Facts
(Analytical components in 100g):

- Energy   173 kcal
- Fat   8.9 g
- Carbohydrate 7.1 g
- Fiber   0.9 g
- Protein   15.8 g

PEANUT BUTTER & BROTH DOG BISCUIT

Ingredients:

- 4.6 oz whole wheat flour (130 g)
- 4.6 oz buckwheat (cooked) (130 g)
- 1.4 oz peanut butter (unsweetened, organic) (40 g)
- ¾ cup bone broth (200 g)
- ¼ tsp rosehip powder (optional)

Nutrition Facts
(Analytical components in 100g):

- Energy   190 kcal
- Fat   5.3 g
- Carbohydrate 26.2 g
- Fiber   4.1 g
- Protein   8.3 g

Preparation:

1. Prepare ingredients at room temperature.
2. Preheat the oven to 356 F (180° C), line the baking tray with parchment paper.
3. Mix the ingredients in a bowl or with the food blender to get a homogeneous "dough". Adjust amounts if needed.
4. Sprinkle whole wheat flour on a rolling board and roll the mixture.
5. Cut treats with knife or cookie cutters and bake for approximately 20 minutes, until golden brown. (Flip biscuits after 10 minutes.)
6. Put them on a rack to cool completely.
7. Store in an airtight container or put them in the freezer to make them last longer.

SWEET & "SPICY" CHIPS

Ingredients:

- 7 oz sweet potato (200 g)
- 1 tsp coconut oil
- ¼ tsp turmeric
- ¼ tsp rosehip powder (optional)

Nutrition Facts
(Analytical components in 100g):

- Energy   90 kcal
- Fat   0.1 g
- Carbohydrate 21.1 g
- Fiber   3.3 g
- Protein   2 g

Preparation:

1. Prepare ingredients at room temperature.
2. Preheat the oven to 392 F (200° C), line the baking tray with parchment paper.
3. Peel and then dice sweet potatoes into big cubes.
4. Mix coconut oil with turmeric and rosehip powder if using, and pour onto the sweet potato.
5. Place sweet potato pieces on the baking tray
6. Bake for approximately 15 minutes, flip the pieces, and bake for another 10 minutes, until golden brown.
7. Put them on a rack to cool completely.
8. Store in an airtight container or put them in the freezer to make them last longer.

OAT & APPLE TREAT

Ingredients:

- 7 oz oat flour (or oatmeal ground to powder) (200 g)
- 1 large egg
- 3.5 oz applesauce (or pureed apple) (100 g)
- ¼ tsp linseed oil (optional)

Preparation:

1. Prepare ingredients at room temperature.
2. Preheat the oven to 347 F (175° C), line the baking tray with parchment paper.
3. Mix the ingredients in a bowl to get a homogeneous "dough". Adjust amounts if needed.
4. Spoon the mixture into muffin tin or oven-safe silicone mold.
5. Bake for approximately 20 minutes, until golden brown.
6. Put them on a rack to cool completely.
7. Store in an airtight container or put them in the freezer to make them last longer.

Nutrition Facts
(Analytical components in 100g):

- Energy   266 kcal
- Fat   6.6 g
- Carbohydrate   41.3 g
- Fiber   4.4 g
- Protein   10.3 g

PUMPIN & OATS TREAT

Ingredients:

- 7 oz oat flour (or oatmeal ground to powder) (200 g)
- 1 large egg
- 3.5 oz pumpkin (can be plain pumpkin puree too) (100 g)
- ¼ tsp linseed oil (optional)

Preparation:

1. Prepare ingredients at room temperature.
2. Preheat the oven to 347 F (175° C), line the baking tray with parchment paper.
3. Mix the ingredients in a bowl to get a homogeneous "dough". Adjust amounts if needed.
4. Spoon the mixture into muffin tin or oven-safe silicone mold.
5. Bake for approximately 20 minutes, until golden brown.
6. Put them on a rack to cool completely.
7. Store in an airtight container or put them in the freezer to make them last longer.

Nutrition Facts
(Analytical components in 100g):

- Energy   257 kcal
- Fat   6.6 g
- Carbohydrate   38.9 g
- Fiber   4 g
- Protein   10.4 g

OVERNIGHT OATS FOR DOGS

Ingredients:

- 7 oz oatmeal (200 g)
- 1 medium, ripe banana
- 1.2 oz peanut butter (unsweetened, organic) (35 g)
- 7 oz yogurt (plain, unsweetened) (200 g)

Preparation:

1. Prepare ingredients at room temperature.
2. Peel and dice banana into tiny cubes.
3. Mix the ingredients in a bowl, until fully combined. Adjust amounts if needed.
4. Pour the mixture into a container and put it in the fridge for 24 hours to let the oatmeal soak up the yogurt.
5. Before serving, let it sit for a while to reach room temperature.
6. Spoon it on top of food, or stuff it into your dog's toy.

Nutrition Facts
(Analytical components in 100g):

- Energy   137 kcal
- Fat   5.7 g
- Carbohydrate   13.6 g
- Fiber   1.6 g
- Protein   3.7 g

SWEET POTATO & CARROT TREAT

Ingredients:

- 7 oz brown rice flour (200 g)
- 5.3 oz sweet potato (cooked, mashed) (150 g)
- 0.7 oz carrot (cooked, mashed) (20 g)
- 1 medium egg
- ¼ tsp rosehip powder (optional)

Preparation:

1. Prepare ingredients at room temperature.
2. Preheat the oven to 347 F (175° C), line the baking tray with parchment paper.
3. Mix the ingredients in a bowl or with the food blender to get a homogeneous "dough". Adjust amounts if needed.
4. Sprinkle brown rice flour on a rolling board and roll the mixture.
5. Cut treats with knife or cookie cutters, and bake for approximately 20 minutes, until golden brown.
6. Put them on a rack to cool completely.
7. Store in an airtight container or put them in the freezer to make them last longer.

Nutrition Facts
(Analytical components in 100g):

- Energy   222 kcal
- Fat   2.7 g
- Carbohydrate   44 g
- Fiber   3.4 g
- Protein   5.7 g

MEAT LOVER TREAT

Ingredients:

- 5.6 oz whole wheat flour (160 g)
- 3.5 oz chicken heart (100 g)
- 1.7 oz chicken liver (50 g)
- 2 medium eggs
- ¼ tsp rosehip powder (optional)

Preparation:

1. Prepare ingredients at room temperature.
2. Preheat the oven to 338 F (170° C), line the baking tray with parchment paper.
3. Clean, then dice liver and heart into big chunks.
4. Mix the ingredients with the food blender to get a homogeneous "dough". Adjust amounts if needed.
5. Spread the mixture on the baking tray.
6. Bake for approximately 20 minutes, until golden brown.
7. Break or cut into pieces.
8. Store in an airtight container or put them in the freezer to make them last longer.

Nutrition Facts
(Analytical components in 100g):

- Energy   221 kcal
- Fat   5.6 g
- Carbohydrate   27.7 g
- Fiber   4.2 g
- Protein   16.9 g

SALMON & PUMPKIN DOG TREAT

Ingredients:

- 7 oz brown rice flour (200 g)
- 3.5 oz salmon (cooked, mashed) (100 g)
- 3.5 oz pumpkin (cooked, mashed) (100 g)
- 3 medium eggs
- ¼ tsp rosehip powder (optional)

Preparation:

1. Prepare ingredients at room temperature.
2. Preheat the oven to 365 F (185° C), line the baking tray with parchment paper.
3. Beat the eggs, then mix the ingredients in a bowl to get a homogeneous "dough". Adjust amounts if needed.
4. Spread the mixture evenly on the baking tray, and bake for 30-40 minutes, until golden brown.
5. Put on a rack to cool completely.
6. Store in an airtight container or put them in the freezer to make them last longer.

Nutrition Facts
(Analytical components in 100g):

- Energy   201 kcal
- Fat   5.1 g
- Carbohydrate   27.9 g
- Fiber   1.9 g
- Protein   9.1 g

SALMON & CARROT DOG TREAT

Ingredients:

- 7 oz brown rice flour (200 g)
- 3.5 oz salmon (cooked, mashed) (100 g)
- 3.5 oz carrot (cooked, mashed) (100 g)
- 3 medium eggs
- ¼ tsp rosehip powder (optional)

Preparation:

1. Prepare ingredients at room temperature.
2. Preheat the oven to 365 F (185° C), line the baking tray with parchment paper.
3. Beat the eggs, then mix the ingredients in a bowl to get a homogeneous "dough". Adjust amounts if needed.
4. Spread the mixture evenly on the baking tray, and bake for 30-40 minutes, until golden brown.
5. Put on a rack to cool completely.
6. Store in an airtight container or put them in the freezer to make them last longer.

Nutrition Facts
(Analytical components in 100g):

- Energy   203 kcal
- Fat   5.1 g
- Carbohydrate   29.4 g
- Fiber   2.3 g
- Protein   9.1 g

LAMB & CARROT TREAT

Ingredients:

- 7 oz brown rice flour (200 g)
- 3.5 oz lamb (cooked, mashed) (100 g)
- 3.5 oz banana (cooked, mashed) (100 g)
- 3 medium eggs
- ¼ tsp rosehip powder (optional)

Preparation:

1. Prepare ingredients at room temperature.
2. Preheat the oven to 365 F (185° C), line the baking tray with parchment paper.
3. Beat the eggs, then mix the ingredients in a bowl to get a homogeneous "dough". Adjust amounts if needed.
4. Spread the mixture evenly on the baking tray, and bake for 30-40 minutes, until golden brown.
5. Put on a rack to cool completely. Break into pieces.
6. Store in an airtight container or put them in the freezer to make them last longer.

Nutrition Facts
(Analytical components in 100g):

- Energy   214 kcal
- Fat   6.8 g
- Carbohydrate   29.4 g
- Fiber   2.3 g
- Protein   9.7 g

CHICKEN & SWEET POTATO TREAT

Ingredients:

- 7 oz brown rice flour (200 g)
- 3.5 oz chicken breast (cooked, mashed) (100 g)
- 3.5 oz sweet potato (cooked, mashed) (100 g)
- 3 medium eggs
- ¼ tsp turmeric (optional)

Preparation:

1. Prepare ingredients at room temperature.
2. Preheat the oven to 365 F (185° C), line the baking tray with parchment paper.
3. Beat the eggs, then mix the ingredients in a bowl to get a homogeneous "dough". Adjust amounts if needed.
4. Spread the mixture evenly on the baking tray, and bake for 30-40 minutes, until golden brown.
5. Put on a rack to cool completely. Break into pieces.
6. Store in an airtight container or put them in the freezer to make them last longer.

Nutrition Facts
(Analytical components in 100g):

- Energy   205 kcal
- Fat   3.5 g
- Carbohydrate 31.7 g
- Fiber   2.3 g
- Protein   11 g

FRUIT MIX PUREE

Ingredients:

- 7 oz watermelon (diced) (200 g)
- 3.5 oz blueberries (100 g)
- 3.5 oz apple (diced) (100 g)
- 7 oz millet (cooked) (200 g)

Preparation:

1. Prepare ingredients at room temperature.
2. Put watermelon, blueberries and apple into a food blender and pulse until fully combined.
3. Add cooked millet to the mixture and pulse again to get a homogenous puree. Remove excess liquid if any. Adjust amounts if needed.
4. Spoon the mixture on top of dog food or use it as an occasional treat or training snack.
5. Store in an airtight container or put it in the freezer to make it last longer.

Nutrition Facts
(Analytical components in 100g):

- Energy   69 kcal
- Fat   0.4 g
- Carbohydrate 15.5 g
- Fiber   1.9 g
- Protein   1.5 g

BLUEBERRY COOKIES

Ingredients:

- 7 oz oat flour (200 g)
- 3 large eggs
- 1 tbsp salmon oil
- 3.5 oz blueberries (mashed) (100 g)
- ¼ tsp rosehip powder (optional)

Nutrition Facts
(Analytical components in 100g):

- Energy   230 kcal
- Fat   7,1 g
- Carbohydrate   32 g
- Fiber   3.4 g
- Protein   10.5 g

Preparation:

1. Prepare ingredients at room temperature.
2. Preheat the oven to 338 F (170° C), line the baking tray with parchment paper.
3. Mix the ingredients in a bowl to get a homogeneous "dough". Adjust amounts if needed.
4. Sprinkle oat flour on a rolling board and roll the mixture.
5. Cut treats with knife or cookie cutters, and bake for approximately 20 minutes, until golden brown.
6. Put them on a rack to cool completely.
7. Store in an airtight container or put them in the freezer to make them last longer.

YOGURT & BACON DOG BISCUIT

Ingredients:

- 8.8 oz oat flour (250 g)
- 1 large eggs
- 3.5 oz yogurt (plain, unsweetened) (100 g)
- 1.7 oz bacon (diced) (50 g)

Nutrition Facts
(Analytical components in 100g):

- Energy   295 kcal
- Fat   10.1 g
- Carbohydrate   36.6 g
- Fiber   3.5 g
- Protein   14.2 g

Preparation:

1. Prepare ingredients at room temperature.
2. Preheat the oven to 338 F (170° C), line the baking tray with parchment paper.
3. Mix the ingredients in a bowl to get a homogeneous "dough". Adjust amounts if needed.
4. Sprinkle oat flour on a rolling board and roll the mixture.
5. Cut treats with knife or cookie cutters, and bake for approximately 20 minutes, until golden brown.
6. Put them on a rack to cool completely.
7. Store in an airtight container or put them in the freezer to make them last longer.

FROZEN TREATS

Frozen treats are great for hot summer days and you can use them as training snacks, too! Due to the fruit-and consequently natural sugar-content of these treats, feed them in moderation.

FROZEN BANANA

Ingredients:

- 3 medium, ripe bananas

Preparation:

1. Cut the banana into cubes and freeze in an ice tray or freezer-safe silicone mold. This is the ultimate quick treat on hot summer days. It's as simple as that!

Nutrition Facts
(Analytical components in 100g):

- Energy   89 kcal
- Fat   0.3 g
- Carbohydrate   23 g
- Fiber   2.6 g
- Protein   1.1 g

PEANUT BUTTER & BANANA

Ingredients:

- 3 medium, ripe bananas
- 0.7 oz peanut butter (sugar-free, organic) (20 g)
- 3.5 oz yogurt (unsweetened, unflavored) (100 g)

Preparation:

1. Puree banana, then mix ingredients in a bowl.
2. Scoop mixture into ice trays or freezer-safe silicone mold and freeze.

Nutrition Facts
(Analytical components in 100g):

- Energy   101 kcal
- Fat   2.6 g
- Carbohydrate   19.2 g
- Fiber   2.1 g
- Protein   2.9 g

PUMPKIN & BANANA

Ingredients:

- 3 medium, ripe bananas
- 3.5 oz pumpkin (baked, pureed, unsweetened) (100 g)

Preparation:

1. Puree banana and pumpkin, and mix well until fully combined.
2. Scoop mixture into ice trays or freezer-safe silicone mold and freeze.

Nutrition Facts
(Analytical components in 100g):

- Energy   70 kcal
- Fat   0.2 g
- Carbohydrate 18 g
- Fiber   2.2 g
- Protein   1 g

FROZEN HEN SOUP

Ingredients:

- 2 ¾ cup water (650 g)
- 5.3 oz chicken thighs (150 g)
- 3.5 oz carrot (100 g)
- 1.7 oz pumpkin (baked) (50 g)
- 1.7 oz apple (50 g)
- 1 tsp rosehip powder (optional)

Preparation:

1. Prepare ingredients at room temperature. Rinse meat carefully. Remove bones from the thighs, leave skin and fat on.
2. Clean thighs carefully if necessary.
3. Cut meat into cubes.
4. Cook meat in water for approximately 15 minutes (amount of water depends on personal preferences) slowly to preserve nutrients.
5. Peel and cut baked pumpkin and carrot into tiny cubes.
6. Add carrot, apple, and pumpkin to the mixture, incorporating it carefully.
7. Pour the mixture into a food processor and mix it to get a homogeneous liquid. You can use a stick blender for mixing.
8. Let the mixture cool down, add rosehip powder, then pour into ice tray or silicone molds and freeze. Perfect training snack on hot summer days!

Nutrition Facts
(Analytical components in 100g):

- Energy   41 kcal
- Fat   2.1 g
- Carbohydrate 2 g
- Fiber   0.5 g
- Protein   3.8 g

FROZEN SPIRULINA CUBE

Ingredients:

- 2 cup bone broth (chicken/turkey/beef/lamb) (500 g)
- 1 tsp spirulina powder (dog-friendly, organic)

Preparation:

1. Prepare ingredients at room temperature.
2. Mix spirulina powder into the bone broth.
3. Pour mixture into ice trays or freezer-safe silicone mold and freeze.

Nutrition Facts
(Analytical components in 100g):

- Energy   16 kcal
- Fat   0.1 g
- Carbohydrate   0.2 g
- Fiber   0 g
- Protein   3.8 g

DESSERT

If you have a sweet tooth, you will love this section! You can make delicious dog-friendly desserts for your canine companion. It is a lot easier than you think! Due to the fruit- and consequently natural sugar-content of these treats, feed them in moderation.

BEETROOT PANCAKE

Ingredients:

- 4.2 oz beetroot (cooked) (120 g)
- 0.7 oz blueberries (20 g)
- 2.1 oz yogurt (unsweetened, unflavored) (60 g)
- 3.5 oz brown rice flour (100 g)

Preparation:

1. Puree cooked beetroot and blueberries.
2. Mix ingredients in a blender or in a bowl until fully combined, set aside. Alternatively, you can use oat flour instead of brown rice flour.
3. Preheat a non-stick pan and fry pancakes until golden brown. You can use a teaspoon of coconut oil for frying to prevent sticking.
4. Let it cool down, and serve, or store in the fridge for 4-5 days or freeze pancakes to make them last longer.

Nutrition Facts
(Analytical components in 100g):

- Energy   158 kcal
- Fat   1.4 g
- Carbohydrate   7.2 g
- Fiber   2.5 g
- Protein   4.2 g

HAM & EGG PUDDING

Ingredients:

- 5 large eggs
- 5.3 oz ham (chopped) (150 g)
- 7 oz yogurt (unsweetened, unflavored) (200 g)

Preparation:

1. Preheat oven to 320 F (160° C)
2. Mix all ingredients in a large bowl until fully combined.
3. Spray muffin tin or oven-safe silicone mold with coconut oil.
4. Fill cups ¾ way and bake until the mixture is fully set (approximately 15-20 minutes, depending on the oven).
5. Let it cool down completely, remove pudding with a spatula.
6. Store in the fridge in an airtight container to make them last longer.

Nutrition Facts
(Analytical components in 100g):

- Energy   116 kcal
- Fat   5.7 g
- Carbohydrate   3 g
- Fiber   0 g
- Protein   12.8 g

BACON & PEAR

Ingredients:

- 3 large pears
- 10.6 oz bacon (sliced) (300 g)

Preparation:

1. Core pear and cut into thin slices.
2. Wrap pear slices with bacon.
3. Place wrapped slices on a baking tray lined with parchment paper.
4. Set the oven to the lowest temperature and bake until crispy. For best results, use a food dehydrator.

Nutrition Facts
(Analytical components in 100g):

- Energy   196 kcal
- Fat   12.1 g
- Carbohydrate   10.1 g
- Fiber   1.9 g
- Protein   12.2 g

BERRY ICE CREAM

Ingredients:

- 7 oz yogurt (200 g)
- 3.5 oz beetroot (cooked) (100 g)
- 0.7 oz banana (20 g)
- 0.7 oz blueberries (20 g)

Preparation:

1. Puree beetroot, blueberries, and banana.
2. Add yogurt to the mixture and mix until fully combined.
3. Scoop mixture into ice tray or popsicle mold and freeze.

Nutrition Facts
(Analytical components in 100g):

- Energy   57 kcal
- Fat   3.2 g
- Carbohydrate   9.3 g
- Fiber   0.9 g
- Protein   3.6 g

DOG FRIENDLY PROTEIN JELLY

Ingredients:

- 3 tbsp unflavored, unsweetened gelatin
- approx. 3 tbsp (45 g) water/soup/broth or fresh apple juice
- +2 tbsp (30 g) water/soup/broth or fresh apple juice for cooking
- ½ tsp spirulina powder

Nutrition Facts
(Analytical components in 100g):

- Energy   161 kcal
- Fat   0.1 g
- Carbohydrate   0.2 g
- Fiber   0.4 g
- Protein   42 g

Preparation:

1. Add natural, plain, unflavored, unsweetened gelatin to cold water/soup/broth/apple juice (no sugar or sweetener!).
2. Let the gelatin "bloom" for a few minutes in the cold liquid.
3. Pour approximately 1 tbsp (15 g) water/soup/borth/apple juice into a bowl and bring it to a boil in the microwave oven.
4. Add bloomed gelatin to the hot liquid and mix thoroughly. Add spirulina powder.
5. Pour the mixture into a silicone mold or ice tray.
6. Put the mold/ice tray into the fridge for at least 2-3 hours until the mixture sets.
7. Keep jelly treats in the fridge, especially on hot summer days.

CONCLUSION

Taking care of your dog is an act of love that teaches us to be responsible for something outside of ourselves. There is nothing that fills our hearts with more joy than seeing our dogs happy, healthy, and full of energy. A good, healthy, and balanced diet is definitely one of the ways we can lovingly accompany them in their lives, just as we do for ourselves. In this book, I tried to provide you with a simple and accessible guide, with tips suitable for days when you have less time as well as for those when you can dedicate more energy and even pamper your four-legged friend in the kitchen.

It's easy to understand why commercial dog food has become so extremely popular: it can be purchased everywhere, it's often very cheap, and therefore it's truly a quick and effective solution, especially for those with busy lives with work, family... But if you now have this book in your hands, it's because you, like me, have realized the negative aspects that come with "easy choices." Commercial dog food too often contains low-quality ingredients, has a serious impact on the health of our planet because it is less sustainable, and obviously, as we all know, can cause a series of long-term health problems for our beloved animals, including intolerances, allergies, and obesity.

Every change requires effort and a bit of sacrifice at first: adding the commitment to cook for your dog to your daily tasks is certainly a challenge, it requires organization and a time, only the love you feel for your dog can give you the right motivation. I have done my best to include clear and simple tips to lighten your load during this transition phase and support you as best as possible. I hope that reading this book will have inspired and encouraged you at least a little bit.

Over time, you will also assimilate those new simple habits that will allow you to save time and money, gaining in quality. You will learn to prepare larger portions at home and store them in the freezer for future use, all already perfectly portioned in the most practical way possible.
I invite you to embrace this new adventure with enthusiasm and curiosity, and to try out the various recipes in my book to discover which ones your dog likes the most.
Cook, have fun, and don't be afraid to make mistakes: you will learn from these and improve more and more. For additional safety, especially at the beginning, don't forget to consult your veterinarian and get help in calculating your furry friend's ideal weight and daily calorie needs to keep him always in the best shape.

Finally, I want to thank you for choosing to take care of your dog in such a loving and attentive way. Every little action and gesture of love we do towards others makes our planet a better place to live in. Animals, our dogs in particular, are proof of how love, joy, and generosity can change the lives of those around us. It's a simple truth that we can experience every day and of which we can become ambassadors with our lifestyle and small daily gestures.

If you enjoyed this guide, if I was helpful to you, I would be immensely grateful to receive your review of the book, it only takes a few moments and it will make a difference in my work. Thank you from the bottom of my heart, and may you and your beloved furry friend have a wonderful life.

METRIC CONVERSION CHART

Oven Temperatures

NO FAN	FAN FORCED	FARENHEIT
120 °C	100 °C	250 °C
150 °C	130 °C	300 °C
160 °C	140 °C	325 °C
180 °C	160 °C	350°C
190 °C	170 °C	375°C
200 °C	180 °C	400°C
230 °C	210 °C	450°C
250 °C	230 °C	500°C

Sr Flour = Self Raising

Cup and Spoons

CUP	METRIC
1/4 cup	60 ml
1/3 cup	80 ml
1/2 cup	125ml
1 cup	250 ml
SPOONS	**SPOONS**
1/4 teaspoon	1.25 ml
1/2 teaspoon	2.5 ml
1 teaspoon	5 ml
2 teaspoon	10 ml
1 Tablespoon	20 ml

Liquids

Cup	Metric	Imperial
	30ml	1 fl oz
1/4 Cup	60ml	2 fl oz
1/3 Cup	80 ml	3 1/2 fl oz
	100 ml	2 3/4 fl oz
1/2 Cup	125 ml	4 fl oz
	150 ml	5 fl oz
3/4 Cup	180 ml	6 fl oz
	200 ml	7 fl oz
1 Cup	250 ml	8 3/4 fl oz
1 1/4 Cups	310 ml	10 1/2 fl oz
1 1/2 Cups	375 ml	13 fl oz
1 3/4 Cups	430 ml	15 fl oz
	475 ml	16 fl oz
2 Cups	500 ml	17 fl oz
2 1/2 Cups	625 ml	21 1/2 fl oz
3 Cups	750 ml	26 fl oz
4 Cups	1L	35 fl oz
5 Cups	1.25L	44 fl oz
6 Cups	1.5L	52 fl oz
8 Cups	2L	70 fl oz
10 Cups	2.5L	88 fl oz

Mass

Imperial	Metric
1/4 oz	10 g
1/2 oz	15 g
1 oz	30 g
2 oz	60 g
3 oz	90 g
4 oz (1/4 lb)	125 g
5 oz	155 g
6 oz	185 g
7 oz	220 g
8 oz (1/2 lb)	250 g
9 oz	280 g
10 oz	315 g
11 oz	345 g
12 oz (3/4 lb)	375 g
13 oz	410 g
14 oz	440 g
15 oz	470 g
16 oz (1 lb)	500 g
24 oz (1 1/2 lb)	750 g
32 oz (2 lb)	1kg
48 oz (3 lb)	1.5kg

DOWNLOAD YOUR GIFT NOW

To download your bonus scan the **QR CODE** below

BONUS

7 NATURAL WAYS TO PAMPER YOUR FURRY FRIEND

SCAN ME or
http://bit.ly/BONUS_Homemade_Dog_Food

LEAVE A SUPER QUICK REVIEW ON AMAZON.COM

Made in the USA
Las Vegas, NV
03 September 2023